FV

The Screwball Comedy Films

A *History and Filmography,*
1934–1942

Duane Byrge
and
Robert Milton Miller

With a Foreword by
ARTHUR KNIGHT

McFarland & Company, Inc., Publishers
Jefferson, North Carolina, and London

Frontispiece: Cary Grant and Katharine Hepburn in *Holiday,* copyright 1938 by Columbia Pictures Corporation.

British Library Cataloguing-in-Publication data are available

Library of Congress Cataloguing-in-Publication Data

Byrge, Duane, 1949–
    The screwball comedy films : a history and filmography, 1934–1942 / Duane Byrge and Robert Milton Miller.
        p.   cm.
    Includes bibliographical references and index.
    ISBN 0-89950-539-2 (lib bdg. : 55# alk. paper) ∞
    1. Comedy films—United States—History and criticism.
    I. Miller, Robert Milton, 1947– . II. Title.
    PN1995.9.C55B97   1991
    791.43′617—dc20   90-52654
                                                                       CIP

Manufactured in the United States of America

McFarland & Company, Inc., Publishers
    Box 611, Jefferson, North Carolina 28640

TABLE OF CONTENTS

FOREWORD

No one who survived the Great Depression of the 1930s can look back on those years with any real affection. In the face of bread lines, Hoovervilles, and hunger marches, few could accept such musical exhortations as *Stand Up and Cheer* ("good times are here") or *We're in the Money* or even *Happy Days Are Here Again*. We may have heard them and whistled them, but we certainly didn't believe them. Not that this lessened the popularity of the movie musicals that propounded them. In those grim days, any ray of hope was worth hanging onto. But the fact is we *knew* those hopes were false and resented them, even though we were loathe to reject them outright. (Interestingly, such overtly Depression numbers as *Ten Cents a Dance* or *Brother, Can You Spare a Dime?* were equally popular with the mass audience.)

Many persist, quite correctly, in seeing the movies as one of the few stabilizing influences during those terrible times. Quite apart from whatever messages they may have delivered (and the "message movie" was every bit as suspect then as it is now), where else could a thin dime buy you not only three hours of escape from economic or domestic woes, but also the physical comfort of a warm place in winter and a cool place in the summer? There were those poor souls who actually used their local picture palaces as short-term flop houses. All this and a double feature as well!

I once wrote that movies, like bananas, come in bunches. Never was this more apparent than in the early years of the Depression, as the film companies fought desperately to hold onto their *nouveau* poor customers. When gangster movies took hold, the studios complied with a veritable deluge of them — 51 in 1931 alone. Then came newspaper stories, prison stories, "true confession" stories, and a sudden rash of backstage musicals featuring hundreds of scantily clad chorus girls in settings more elaborate than any theatre since Rome's Colosseum could possibly contain. By their very nature, these cycles tended to be intensive but short-lived. Even the entertainment-hungry audiences of the Depression could become sated by too much of a good thing.

What Duane Byrge and Robert Milton Miller remind us in this scrupulously researched volume is that, unlike previous cycles and genres, screwball comedy was not an overnight phenomenon, nor did it arrive fully blown and ready for instant Xeroxing. Perhaps that also explains its relatively long hold on the public, roughly from 1934 to 1942. During those years, the whole idea of screwball was constantly changing, defining itself more as an attitude than as a specific type of subject. Significantly, the term itself wasn't even invented until a year or so after the genre had begun . . .

It Happened One Night, on the only hand, even though it came at the end of a rather dreary succession of romances that took place on a bus, immediately commanded attention because its outlook was so markedly different. An heiress runs away from her marriage to a stuffed shirt. A sardonic newspaper man is (at least at first) less interested in the girl than in the reward — and his story. It is only when both of them discover that, despite their differences in social and economic status, they are really very human beings that the walls of Jericho begin to crumble. Even the girl's crusty multi-millionaire father turns out to be human. And audiences loved it, loved them.

For me, that's the whole secret of the screwball's success. Its rich people were always human — if also somewhat fatuous. It was an image that both delighted and enheartened the impoverished and hungry. As with Chaplin, it was the rich seen from the perspective of the poor, and with the same often hilarious results. One always enjoys seeing the wealthy brought down a peg, the weaknesses of the powerful exposed. If they can be made human as well, they become more credible, more believable, and hence more effective as symbols of a class that was both hated and envied in the Depression years. The irony is that, invariably, sympathy was built up for these irascible moguls (usually played by the likes of Edward Arnold, Walter Connolly, and Eugene Pallette), so much so that by the end of the movie the audiences were more than willing to forgive and forget their overbearing ways. They were, after all, only human.

Nor is it a coincidence that most of the screwball comedies — and certainly most of the more successful — were played out against backgrounds of sheer opulence. Park Avenue penthouses, luxury hotels, and Connecticut estates abounded, as if to remind Depression audiences not merely that such places still existed, but that with a little bit of luck (the kind of luck visited upon the heroes and heroines of these films), they might be theirs as well. For a people who have always believed in luck, and what anthropologist Hortense Powdermaker once called the "Magic Helper," these films served as a palliative to the grim realities that surrounded them and as a counter to the growing sense of desperation that was sweeping the land during the 1930s. I might add, I have often wondered just how much of this was calculated by their producers. Certainly, once the Depression was over, so were the screwballs.

But that is for the sociologists to figure out. As Byrge and Miller emphasize in this text, these were primarily "feel good" movies, made with an *élan* that extended beyond their attractive stars and scintillating sets to the directors, writers, and producers who created them. The films had an infectious sense of fun about them, and a saucy sexiness that often seemed barely to skirt the rigid proscriptions of the MPAA's Production Code. More than any films before the (or even since), they depicted an equality between the sexes, the give-and-take of equals, a sense of camaraderie that quite transcended the conventions of boy-meets-girl. The dialogue was witty and sophisticated, the casting frequently superb, the outlook anarchistic. They were the perfect escapist entertainment.

It may be difficult to believe, as you read through the detailed synopses offered in this book, that these sparkling scripts were actually concocted during one of the grimmest periods this nation has ever known. But there lies the true miracle of screwball!

Arthur Knight

INTRODUCTION

What we now think of as the classic screwball comedy flourished during only a brief, but highly creative segment of American film history. This fleeting subgenre was popular during the "New Deal" portion of the Great Depression, beginning just a few years after the birth of the sound film. Less than a decade later, in the midst of wartime optimism and unity of national purpose, the joyously anarchic screwball comedy receded from the interests of film makers and the public alike. When the war was over, the insouciant elegance of high 1930s comedy, including its screwball variation, had become an outdated style and approach, something to be as scrupulously avoided by the "new" Hollywood as prewar hairstyles, clothes, music, and cars. Yet the screwball comedy left its mark on the movie cognoscenti, and elements of this entrancing movie madness would eventually turn up, like avatars of a golden age, in much later productions.

At first the revival was in name only, with a mid-1950s cycle of humorless remakes of the best-remembered films — surely a desperate attempt to "bring back the magic" by the giant studios who still owned the original titles and stories. A generation later, uncredited plot twists, gags, and characterizations with screwball origins began to appear in independently packaged sex comedies of the 1970s and 1980s. These were largely the creation of younger film makers whose liberal arts education, formally or avocationally, had included generous doses of the classics — of the screen. But such latter-day imitations, even the best of them, remain either sincere homages or crude ripoffs, devoid of the censor-confounding, Depression-denying sensibility which gave the genuine article its subversive charm and absurdist authority.[1]

Thanks first to late-night television, then to museums, film societies and revival theaters, and most recently to pay-cable and home video, the witty riches of the screwball era are still with us, however, readily available for sampling or even gorging by the comedy-hungry viewer of today. This book is intended as an historical menu for the feast, as well as a guide to sorting out and identifying the certifiably screwball from the much larger parade of vintage cinema comedy which surrounds it in the program schedules and on the cassette racks. Each of the feature films described in the second section of this book has been found by the authors to qualify as sufficiently "screwy," by the standards of the era, to merit inclusion in our annotated filmography. And while the total number of films we cover, when viewed against the statistical backdrop of a time when the major studios together released at least one new picture every day, looks rather small, it can take on enormous cultural weight when coupled with the historical consensus that it is the screwball comedy which is most often evoked by writers seeking to represent the style and sensibility of 1930's American movies in general.

The special fictional characters of screwball differed from the legions of their more ordinary admirers, relaxing in the plush seats of the darkened movie palaces, in so many ways—yet at a deeper level the similarities to the very persons those viewers had once been were striking, for the middle-to-upper-class, smartly dressed, and verbally deft pretty folk on the screen defied the social proprieties of their class and culture in the innocently aggressive, noisily silly, endearingly defiant, and happily destructive way that little children at play repeatedly disturb the peace and boredom of adults' vain attempts to maintain domestic tranquility. In short, the screwball comedy pleased the movie-going public by combining slapstick with sophistication, as characters who supposedly had ample reason to follow strict social convention took leave of at least some measure of their comfortable sanity and reverted to childish pranks while in evening dress, unabashedly wearing their egos on their sleeves while verbally sparring to the tune of *New Yorker*-style *bon mots* or gleefully allowing pushes to turn to shoves in the most literal fashion. Not only was it great fun while it lasted, but a half-century later the high-fashion hi-jinks, though stripped by time of their sex-and-class-struggle immediacy, amazingly still amuse—surely a tribute to the comedic skill of their creators.

Like most Hollywood product then and now, a screwball comedy was at heart a love story. Its central romance was frequently instigated by an aggressive, even eccentric woman whose efforts to prod her more stodgy and conventional beau along the rocky road to the altar primed the comic mechanisms for a great deal of humor-by-embarrassment. Improbable events, mistaken identities, and ominously misleading circumstantial evidence quickly compounded upon each other, albeit by seemingly logical progression, until a frantic conclusion in which even the impending marriage gives only faint promise of providing some whit of order as antidote to the previous narrative chaos.

Difficulties in reconciling romantic leads' eccentricities were commonly complicated by other seemingly insurmountable obstacles to their union. Rules, customs, family obligations, romantic rivals—all needed to be circumvented, disregarded, or superseded, often with a cheery vengeance. Even lovers who were portrayed as highly intelligent could have lapses of silliness and mischief when temporarily confounded by the dull nature of their social station's conventions. Some screwball comedies were also comedies of remarriage, allowing the damaged union of the opening reel to be strengthened or replaced via the invigoration of a screwball interlude in the center of the story.[2] Screwball couples whose relationship was not threatened throughout the narrative might instead be on a mission of some sort, perhaps to solve a mystery, and their odd-even pairing actually strengthened them in conquering the improbable and complicating obstacles they eagerly encountered in racing to the riotous, or at least crazily baffling, last reel.

Life for much of the original audience of these films was undeniably hard. The screwball fantasy offered to them on the screen implied that life should be fun, echoing the playtime standard of childhood. Jobs that made one a slave to a time schedule or mates who put happiness secondary to wealth and social position were scorned by the screwball ethic. The "real world" depicted in the fantasy was ultimately nonsensical. Yet it was a more appealing world than the one outside the theater's doors, for the pretend world's threats could be anarchically overcome by cheeky misbehavior, besting oppression by regression. There was but scant acknowledgment of a continuing economic crisis or approaching war in screwball comedy, and the traditional bridges to achievement and happiness were only temporarily blocked. Passage and liberation were still possible. When the screwball hero and heroine took on the world, they did so not in a crusade of reform, but in a delirious spirit of self-survival, in some measure creating in the process a new and private world of their own devising. What admiration they commanded from the typical audience member was due in part to the marvelous independence they displayed in regard to their surroundings.

Screwball comedy generated part of its dramatic interest from subverting historic and contemporary class conflicts, subsuming them into the disarming dialectic of sexual attraction versus sexual tension. If one of the lovers was from a lower class than the other, their very social polarities enhanced their state of sexual differentiation; the opposites attracted in more ways than one. The characters' ultimate pairing at narrative's end transmitted a unifying illusion to the audience which was welcome during a time of potential social division. Individual self-assertion was championed in these films, and even screwball lovers from distant sides of the tracks ultimately concurred in their opposition to depersonalizing social institutions. Each time love in screwball comedy succeeded in conquering all that had opposed it, another blow was struck for transcendence of class and custom. Of course, the singleness of purpose with which the screwball rich pursued their romantic goals in defiance of a rigid society could also be identified as parodically characteristic of the spoiled child of wealth who learns early on that "no" need never be taken for an answer. Yet screwball comedy displayed this defiant determination to have-fun-at-any-price with more admiration than disdain because it was an integral part of an over-arching fantasy that connected deeply with the tarnished hopes and dreams of an audience who willingly spent even their last spare change for another artificial glimpse at a kinder and funnier world.

Before the parade begins, we offer an overview of the major screwball artists, those performers, writers and directors most responsible for the treasure trove that is their celluloid bequest to us.

MAJOR PERFORMERS

By the end of its Depression-era run, the screwball comedy cycle had played host to quite a few of the American film industry's star performers. Some, like Bette Davis, Fredric March, Robert Montgomery, Jean Harlow, James Cagney, Errol Flynn, Olivia de Havilland, or Gary Cooper, appeared in screwball only once or twice during their illustrious careers. Others, such as Katharine Hepburn, Joel McCrea, Barbara Stanwyck, Constance Bennett, or William Powell, appeared two or three times and even to high acclaim, but are primarily remembered for their long string of successes in different, or related genres. But there are certain stars who returned to the screwball fold again and again, firmly entwining their names and images with the overall historic impression of this remarkable group of motion pictures. The actors and actresses who appeared most frequently and to the greatest and most lasting effect in screwball comedy often did so only after achieving stardom in more conventional fare. The cycle's eight-year run generated few new stars from the ranks of the unknown, but it did rejuvenate several careers and assist in extending the length of others.

Screwball's grandest success story is that of Cary Grant, a former child acrobat from Britain, who left his troupe's tour of America to act and sing in stage musicals. From 1932 to 1936 he was a Paramount-contracted leading man in various genres, seemingly cast more for his looks than his charm. A determination to pick his own parts motivated him to negotiate a non-exclusive arrangement with RKO and Columbia thereafter, and in 1937 he had the good fortune to appear in a pair of consecutive screwball hits: *Topper* (free-lancing for Hal Roach as a cocktail-sipping ghost) and Leo McCarey's *The Awful Truth* (as an errant husband determined to reclaim his nearly divorced wife). This style of comedy brilliantly matched Grant's ability to deliver witty lines with a unique mixture of angst, amusement and elan, and he was soon in great demand to repeat that performance style in similar films.

Director Howard Hawks, in pursuing his *Twentieth Century* vision of having attractive leading players do the kind of physical humor once reserved for eccentric comics, then found Grant ideal for the part of a flustered dinosaur-researcher in *Bringing Up Baby* (1938). Although Katharine Hepburn's uninhibitedly aggressive, female prankster-pursuer proved to be too extreme in its liberated looniness for contemporary tastes, Grant's endearingly passive-but-flustered male won him still greater industry recognition as the movies' new farceur of choice. Director George Cukor, who had unsuccessfully paired Grant with Hepburn two years earlier in the disastrous *Sylvia Scarlett*, then gave the pair another try in the mildly screwball *Holiday* (1938), resulting in an appealingly enthusiastic performance from the actor as a young Wall-Street success who switches fiancées en route to escaping the Gotham rat race. Even in high-minded adventure films such as *Gunga Din* and *Only Angels Have Wings* (both 1939) Grant found himself able to leaven his obvious romantic appeal with occasional displays of controlled, comic hesitation and sly, self-mockery.

Hawks pushed a willing Grant over the edge of customary cinematic restraint in the verbally explosive *His Girl Friday* (1940), to the effect that his driving and devious editor character becomes a Vesuvius of screwball invective, imperiousness and petty intrigue. His romantic motivation—to win back his former wife/star reporter—not only justifies the editor's crazed behavior, but is in turn itself justified by the Hollywood logic implicit in Grant's romantic countenance and presence. That same year Grant excelled in an *Awful Truth* reworking called *My Favorite Wife*, yet another screwball classic about a disrupted marriage comically reconstructed to the mutual delight of its fictional participants and real-life viewers.

Before the cycle waned, Grant managed to score one more time—in Cukor's elegant *Philadelphia Story* (1940), as the perplexed ex-husband of an "ice goddess" (Katharine Hepburn as an overly cultured, socially perfect, Main-Line heiress). He wins her back from an impending remarriage after a revealing, pre-nuptial encounter with the working press. Subsequently Grant lent his by-then practiced comic expertise to a pair of quasi-screwball gems, the fervently sentimental *Penny Serenade* (1941) and the Capra-like social comedy

The Talk of the Town (1942), both under the guidance of the director who had elicited Grant's memorable Cockney-soldier performance in *Gunga Din*, George Stevens.

Grant was reunited with Leo McCarey for one of the cycle's closing efforts, the oddly uneven *Once Upon a Honeymoon* (1942), as an American secret agent whose recruitment of a Nazi official's new bride turns to dangerous romance on the high seas. Although the picture did little to advance the actor's esteem as the definitive screwball male, so secure was Grant's hold on the unofficial title that he was the key asset on which Howard Hawks built two highly amusing but generally uninfluential revivals of the genre in the post-war era, *I Was a Male War Bride* (1948) and *Monkey Business* (1952).

In attempting to assess what there was about this actor which adapted so well to screwball comedy, the most convincing answer seems to be found in Grant's synthesis of contradictory aspects. His pronounced good looks, which unlike so many other performers actually improved as he entered his mid-30s and began his string of screwball performances, were those of a conventional screen hero, but his characterizations were often marked by lapses in composure, self-confidence, personal resolve, and even civility or dexterity. He could be the picture of style and wit in one scene, then take a pratfall, be reduced to stuttering exasperation, or bark and whinny at the source of his problems in the next. In effect, Grant's ability to function simultaneously as a romantic lead and as a genuinely comic figure helped define the de facto standards of casting and performance for screwball comedy. Furthermore, the visible insecurity beneath the polished exterior of his movie image may have appeared convincing (despite his limited acting range) in part because of the serious emotional turmoil of his personal life, as revealed by several latter-day biographers. Grant's amazingly long career as a leading man (1932-66) encompassed many more films outside the screwball cycle, but it is with those very special films that his name continues closely to be linked.[3]

The actress who shares equal distinction with Grant in personifying the screwball spirit and style had a much briefer career (due to premature death) but also began feature stardom as a Paramount contractee. Carole Lombard, like Cary Grant, toiled for several years in films of various genres before reaching top-rank status in screwball comedy. A hard-working and ambitious actress from her early teens, Lombard was a thorough professional, having "paid her dues" in a wide variety of pictures by the time of her screwball breakthrough in one of the founding films of the genre, Howard Hawks' *Twentieth Century* (1934).

Numerous biographical accounts depict her as Hollywood's beautiful tomboy, a tough-talking but vivacious charmer, adored by virtually all of her coworkers on both sides of the camera. The practical-joking, impulsively outspoken aspects of her personality had been confined to her offscreen life until Hawks merged them into her role of the hot-tempered actress who verbally battles her flamboyant ex-director/lover (John Barrymore) in the successful filming of Hecht and MacArthur's rowdy stage play. The winning combination of attractiveness and eccentricity which gave screwball comedy its fresh appeal has been repeatedly tracked back to Lombard's delightfully enraged performance as stage star Lily Garland, but it was not until five films later, in Mitchell Leisen's *Hands Across the Table* (1935) that another screwball opportunity, and a more restrained one at that, beckoned.

Lombard's portrayal of a money-minded manicurist who finds love in a garret was more screwball in its approach to gold digging than in her performance per se, but her polished skill at romantic comedy in general blended well with the story and proved a stepping stone to the triple triumphs of *My Man Godfrey* (1936), *True Confession* (1937), and *Nothing Sacred* (1937), which established her as the female embodiment of the screwball sensibility in movies. In fact, it was a critic's borrowing of a baseball term, in reviewing the first of these, which coined the "screwball comedy" designation — responding to Lombard's portrayal of a spoiled heiress' screamingly funny, albeit dizzy, bratty, and thoughtless behavior when she brings home a supposed "bum" and installs him as the new butler in the family mansion. The second film scored with audiences in large measure due to her memorable performance as an endearingly compulsive liar, whose phony murder confession wreaks havoc with the justice system. The third picture gave Lombard a wide berth in which to shine as another truthless and wide-eyed "innocent," this time allowing a crass newspaperman to exploit ruthlessly the mistaken story of her impending death from radium poisoning.

The busy actress surrounded these screwball masterpieces with several other fine performances in standard romantic comedy and drama of the late 1930s and the turn of the decade. Then she made what became her last screwball appearance, in a film surprisingly directed by thrill-master Alfred Hitchcock, *Mr. and Mrs. Smith* (1941). While not on the dizzying plane of zany and impulsive behavior which typified the cycle at its height, Lombard's performance was nevertheless very effective in this sharp-edged Norman Krasna story of a couple's troubled re-courtship after learning their "perfect" marriage is not legal.

Lombard's subsequent and final performance, before losing her life in a plane crash the following year, was for the screen's master of sophisticated comedies of manners, Ernst Lubitsch. *To Be or Not to Be*, while primarily a mixture of political satire (a troupe of Polish actors trick the Nazis) and the director's unique style of clever sexual innuendo, benefited greatly from Lombard's screwball-honed sense of comic timing and line delivery. The grim realities of later war news, plus the picture's posthumous release following her tragic accident, cast an undeserved pall over the film which faded only with its widely applauded revival several years later. Lombard perished on a return flight to Hollywood from a successful war-bond sales tour, and her disappearance from the screen closely and symbolically presaged the departure of the very comedy style which, despite her success in other genres, she had come to represent. It has been nearly impossible for latter-day writers to invoke the memory of screwball comedy without mentioning her name, and anyone who takes the opportunity to view her best work, despite the passage of a half-century, will immediately see why.[4]

Just as the rise of screwball greatly boosted the career of Cary Grant, it also elevated the screen status of the ever-urbane Melvyn Douglas, whose early years in Hollywood as a Goldwyn contractee had been spent almost exclusively on loan-out with meager success. A seasoned stage performer, Douglas might have returned permanently to Broadway had he not scored a genuine hit as the repressed title character liberated by Claudette Colbert's dutiful secretary in Columbia's *She Married Her Boss* (1935). Douglas' assured gift for sly sophistication mixed with an impish sense of amusement won him the same sort of non-exclusive arrangement with that studio that Grant would also parlay to continuing screwball success, only in Douglas' case he split his Columbia time for the next seven years with other assignments primarily at MGM instead of RKO.

The performance which led Metro executives to offer so much work to one of their non-exclusives was the actor's second screwball smash for Columbia, *Theodora Goes Wild* (1936), in which his portrayal of Irene Dunne's chagrined commercial-artist/liberator matched her own clever star-turn exceedingly well. Nevertheless, much of Douglas' frequent screen work in the latter half of the decade was in either conventional romantic drama or in *Thin Man*-style mysteries. However, his ego-inflated suitor in Paramount's *I Met Him in Paris* (1937) was another hilarious contribution to the screwball cycle, then at its peak.

The comedy classic for which Douglas is best remembered was less screwball than political satire overlaid with the comedy of manners, but his mastery of the "battle of the sexes" banter with Greta Garbo in the Ernst Lubitsch-MGM *Ninotchka* (1939) is clearly of an extended piece with Douglas' finest efforts in the cycle under study here. That same year he also did the solidly screwball *Good Girls Go to Paris* for Alexander Hall at Columbia and excelled as a bemused British professor, pursued in America by Joan Blondell's social-climbing ex-waitress. Douglas' next screwball picture was *Too Many Husbands* (1940), part of that group of multiple variations on the comic love triangle of *The Awful Truth* in which a spare spouse or accidental case of bigamy spurs the plot. In this case the unexpectedly flattered-and-courted wife (Jean Arthur) gets to choose (and just barely does) between worldly Douglas and homespun Fred MacMurray.

Although Lubitsch's first authentically screwball effort, *Bluebeard's Eighth Wife* (1938), had misfired from the miscasting of non-sophisticate Gary Cooper as the male lead, the director's success with Douglas the following year did at least inspire the master to approach the borders of the genre again in 1941. The result was the psychologically bizarre *That Uncertain Feeling*, in which polished farceur Douglas dithers and schemes while playing an upper-class husband (to chic Merle Oberon) with growing misgivings about how to react to his neglected wife's blossoming affair with a flamboyant, possibly psychotic, concert pianist (Burgess Meridith).

Although the premise of *Our Wife* (1941), with its masquerade, for business reasons, of a non-existent marriage would seem most appropriately screwball even without Douglas in the cast, the goings-on lack the requisite social bite and credible sexual tension, veering off instead into conventional farce. The actor did, however, participate one more time in the screwball cycle before it faded with the arrival of the war. The picture was titled *Two-Faced Woman* (1942), and it re-teamed him with Garbo, his *Ninotchka* costar. Douglas was in splendid form as a "possibly" deceived husband attempting to seduce his own wife—while she pretends to be her non-existent, more liberated sister. MGM's re-editing of the finished film, to placate angry censors who saw Douglas' character as remorselessly attempting adultery, only succeeded in raising the narrative's confusion level. In any case, the leading lady's radical departure from her more exotic screen image so distressed her fans that dissatisfaction with the production was even more widespread. Its boxoffice failure helped ring down the curtain on screwball.[5]

While both Melvyn Douglas and Cary Grant had long acting careers which extended well beyond the screwball cycle, the perennially youthful Grant continued as a romantic film star until his 1966 retirement to the cosmetics business. Douglas spent the 1950s primarily as a successful stage and live television actor. It was only in the mid-1960s that he flourished in a new series of screen roles, but these intense characterizations of senior citizens were a far cry from the well dressed, highly confident, and wryly self-amused partnering he had once provided to many of the 1930s most glamorous leading ladies. Douglas at the height of his movie career had consistently appeared more worldly wise and mature than his true age (he did not reach 40 until 1941), but his latter-day return to film acting displayed him as appearing quite advanced in years. Nevertheless, his ever-present trace of a smirk, disarming even the most serious antagonists in a dramatic situation, can still be glimpsed in his final performances as a direct reminder of his supreme mastery of comfortable nonchalance and well-to-do mischief making on the movie screens of long ago.

Irene Dunne's dual success in musical comedy and sentimental drama pre-dated her standout performances in the screwball cycle, and even without that third phase of her career, her place in Hollywood history would still be secure. The marvelous extension of her acting range began with *Theodora Goes Wild* (1936), which led to her non-exclusive pact with Columbia. Up to that point Dunne had impressed the public essentially by means of her superbly trained voice and resolutely cheerful dignity under dramatic stress. She had played conventional musical comedy on stage since her late teens, and her early sound-film years had also given her the chance to emote effectively in some highly popular "weepies," the best known of which are *Back Street* (1932) and *Magnificent Obsession* (1935). It was only at age 32, when she was approaching the end of a long line of trilling ingenues and forced-to-grow up heroines, that she pleasingly startled moviegoers as a small-town author/spinster who "goes wild" on a New York trip originally intended for a business meeting with the publisher of her secretly written, scandalous romance novels. In the picture's Mary McCarthy story, under

Stanislavsky method director Richard Boleslawsky, Dunne revealed a new level of self-satirical, infectious good humor in mildly absurd situations. She beautifully matched the comparable playing of Melvyn Douglas as her commercial artist "liberator," and *Theodora Goes Wild* became a big hit.

Columbia tried to repeat that accomplishment the following year, with Dunne as the female lead in Leo McCarey's chaotically improvised but hugely successful *The Awful Truth*. Paired with Cary Grant as an estranged couple on the eve of their divorce, she delivered another astonishingly funny performance, particularly in the prized sequence in which she drops her good-natured dignity to crash a family gathering at the home of her spouse's intended new wife. Dunne's characterization of a well-bred woman's satirical impersonation of a naïvely lewd cabaret chanteuse even topped Dunne's hilarious *Theodora* role as a proper lady author who pretends to assume the egregious lifestyle of her novel's sexually adventurous heroine.

A less boisterous screwball project at RKO in 1938, *Joy of Living*, gave Dunne a fine battle-of-the-sexes romance onscreen with Douglas Fairbanks, Jr., tinged with some pointed satire of the backstage Broadway musical milieu in which she had thrived prior to heading west in 1930. In 1939, still at RKO but once again under the genially informal direction of McCarey, Dunne gave a stellar performance in an extraordinary picture which combined the tear-jerking, heavy sentiment of her early films with a few leavening touches of screwball sensibility in the early scenes of attempted seduction by a world-class playboy (Charles Boyer). Although the film has been out of authorized circulation for a half-century, *Love Affair* remains, to those fortunate enough to have seen it, the peak of Dunne's non-screwball career.

Dunne's fortuitous relationship with McCarey continued, despite his convalescence following a car crash, in his subsequent and wholly screwball production (directed by McCarey associate Garson Kanin) of *My Favorite Wife* (1940), in which a new comic marital triangle is structured around a flustered husband (Cary Grant) whose remarriage plans are interrupted by the reappearance of the wife he thought was lost at sea. Dunne's gift for insinuating playful chinks in her armor of sensible behavior comes to the fore as she earnestly informs/torments her spouse with maddeningly incomplete details of her being marooned on an island with a handsome "Adam" (Randolph Scott) to her "Eve."

Deliberately alternating the serious with the screwball, Dunne continued her output of multiple handkerchief dramas in this time period, such as *Invitation to Happiness* (1939), *When Tomorrow Comes* (1939), and *Penny Serenade* (1941) — the latter a George Stevens directed tear-fest which successfully employed Dunne's comedic skills to relieve the stresses of a superior domestic tragedy. Her final contributions to the screwball era at last united her with another of its masters, director Gregory La Cava, but at Universal they turned out a pair of less successful comic romances, *Unfinished Business* (1941) and *Lady in a Jam* (1942). Hampered dually by the waning of the screwball cycle and by La Cava's growing reliance upon improvisation to the neglect of plot construction and audience response, the first project mixed serious, even psychological concerns with what might have been a top-rank screwball triangle involving the leading lady and two disparate brothers. The second film had Dunne's character consulting an analyst — who disdains her madcap behavior.

The doubly serious entities of wartime and an approaching fortieth birthday led Dunne away from the frivolous world of screwball comedy. She raised homefront spirits in patriotic deluges of sentiment such as *A Guy Named Joe* (1943) and *The White Cliffs of Dover* (1944), then warmly endorsed the family values of postwar America in the nostalgia gilded *I Remember Mama* (1947) and *Life with Father* (1948). The wholly sensible and idealized Dunne of her post-screwball films had moved so far from her late 1930s "wildness" that in 1950 she overwhelmingly assumed the mantle of age and austerity to portray elderly Queen Victoria in *The Mudlark*. Retirement from the screen came two years later, when Irene Dunne was 48.[6]

If Carole Lombard was the epitome of daffiness on the screwball screen and Irene Dunne cornered the market on temporary abandonment of dignity, Claudette Colbert took the honors for cleverness and determination. Like Lombard and Dunne, Colbert had been playing leads in major studio pictures for half a decade before joining the screwball parade. Her transition to the genre actually put her at the procession's auspicious beginning, winning a 1934 Academy Award for her runaway heiress in Frank Capra's *It Happened One Night*. Impetuous, stubborn, self-impressed and hopelessly spoiled, her character, in romantic conflict with the down-to-earth reporter (Clark Gable) who befriends and exploits her, helped set the style for both the battle-of-the-sexes and the cross-class conflict variations of screwball comedy for the rest of the decade.

One of many Broadway performers scooped up by Hollywood's early-talkie talent raid, Colbert's expert ability to play comedy was at first camouflaged amidst a wide assortment of roles at Paramount or on loan. Apart from the Capra film it is her overtly sexy performances in De Mille's *The Sign of the Cross* (1932) and *Cleopatra* (1934) which are best-known from Colbert's early years of stardom. (Her fine work for Lubitsch in 1931's *The Smiling Lieutenant* remains — as of this writing — shamefully imprisoned, at taxpayer expense, in an archive.) Even when her comedic skill was crowned with a surprise Oscar, Colbert followed the same even-handed path as Lombard and Dunne, attempting to retain her credentials as a serious actress via alternating comedies with dramas and by insisting upon script approval.

Colbert's second appearance in a screwball comedy, *The Gilded Lily* (1935), featured her in a much more docile part than the feisty one she had undertaken for Capra. Her working-girl character's obedient assumption of manufactured celebrity status (woven by her reporter boyfriend out of her erstwhile and fleeting romance with a nobleman) marked the last time for many years that Colbert would play the passive role in comedy of any stripe. Her personal secretary character in *She Married Her Boss* (1935) successfully takes over both the family and business fortunes of Melvyn Douglas' compliant executive, and her shopgirl on holiday in *I Met Him in Paris* (1937) coyly plays the attentions of two determined suitors against each other in a protractedly funny game of romantic rivalry with an Alpine resort setting. Even in the primarily non-screwball *The Bride Comes Home* (1935), released between the two previous titles, Colbert's character remains in control — as an ex-heiress (now impoverished) still fending off the attentive men.

So successful a comedienne was Colbert by the time of her second picture with the great Lubitsch, *Bluebeard's Eighth Wife* (1938), that even the master of sophisticated screen suggestiveness was motivated to direct a screwball vehicle for her. Darker in emotional tone than previous entries in the genre, the narrative presents Colbert as not just an amusingly determined young woman, but as a dollar driven doll whose new marriage to a possibly Landru-like millionaire nearly founders from what appears to be her connivance to drive him insane. The golddigger inclination of Colbert's character in that picture was softened, but still present the next year in the superbly screwball *Midnight*, scripted by the same team as *Bluebeard* (Billy Wilder and Charles Brackett) but directed instead by romanticist

Mitchell Leisen. Colbert's French birth and bilingual/cultural identity (she emigrated to the U.S. at age five) had received indirect reference in the settings and dialogue of several of her previous films, and *Midnight* continued the practice in a Cinderella inspired story of an American showgirl stranded in France. Her determination to snare a wealthy admirer, after rebuffing the attentions of a penniless taxi driver, lands her at a swank Parisian social gathering, where a scheming gentleman impulsively decides to sponsor her party crashing, upper class nose tweaking masquerade.

It's a Wonderful World (1940), a rare Colbert performance for MGM, does reveal some definite couple-on-the-run inspiration from *It Happened One Night,* but the anarchic tilt of the screwball vision is secondary to the emphasis on adventure. It was not until 1942, at the close of the cycle, that Colbert made her next, and final, appearance in the genre—closing out the era just as magnificently, if not influentially, as she had helped initiate it eight years earlier. In *The Palm Beach Story* she again portrays a money-minded female, but this time her character is already married. Her frustration grows out of her inability to assist her failed-inventor husband in backing his fantastic architectural aspirations. In the perverse logic of screwball, she resolves benignly to divorce him and go fortune hunting for a millionaire backer, using her shapely self as bait.

Colbert's forthright, bright and determined style of performance, even when delivering the tortuously funny dialogue of writer-director Preston Sturges, was the direct opposite of the scatter-brained Lombard or the proper versus wild Dunne at either of her modal extremes. The Colbert character functioned most often in screwball with obvious and extroverted intelligence, just as she did in drama or romantic comedy. In a Colbert screwball comedy, it was the setting, the situation, or the subsidiary players who provided the eccentricities. Like Irene Dunne (and probably Carole Lombard, if she had lived), Claudette Colbert moved on to patriotic schmaltz of a high order, during wartime, and met the screen challenge of middle age with postwar domestic roles. Like Melvyn Douglas, Colbert retreated to the stage and television as the old Hollywood faded from view in the 1950s, and even in her senior citizen years she continued to act on occasion, impressing critics as a still glamorous, long term survivor from the movies' golden era.[7]

While each of the previously examined performers were already established as leading players before their excursions into screwball comedy, Fred MacMurray stands out as an exception to this pattern.

A dance-band saxophonist whose vocalizing with Gus Arnheim's orchestra in the late 1920s led to featured parts in a few Broadway musicals, MacMurray was only a fresh recruit to Paramount's stable of talent when Claudette Colbert saw his screen test and requested him as her costar in *The Gilded Lily* (1935). So appealing were his tall good looks and unpretentious Midwestern manner that he was soon partnering several more of Hollywood's top draw actresses in a veritable stream of romantic comedies and adventures. Most of these mainstream productions were, of course, non-screwball. *The Gilded Lily* most definitely was screwball, however, with its clever barbs against both the upper class and the media. MacMurray was quite effective as the scheming reporter and publicity maven who crafts Colbert's character into the personification of a public non-event—a talentless "entertainer" made famous via her much touted "rejection" of a nobleman (Ray Milland, also cast in his first big Paramount part).

Four films later, and still that same year, MacMurray was back in screwball and once more playing the no-nonsense Midwesterner who turns the head of a working girl (this time Carole Lombard) away from a rich but unsuitable suitor. The film was *Hands Across the Table,* and its success confirmed MacMurray's: His surprising charm seems to have stemmed from the assuredness with which he could portray the "average guy." Two years (and ten more films) down the road, his character's restrained panic attacks in the face of Lombard's fine-tuned displays of frenzy made him an excellent foil for her again, when she scored as the chronic liar and alleged murderess his character naïvely defends in the boisterously cynical *True Confession* (1937).

At this point in his career MacMurray branched out into his first movie musicals and even played sentimental drama, but he returned to screwball at its second home—Columbia—for the comic/romantic triangle of *Too Many Husbands* (1940). Jean Arthur was the enjoyably flattered spouse, busily setting up roadblocks to the boudoir destinations of rivals MacMurray and Melvyn Douglas, who by this point in the screwball cycle had, with MacMurray, become the only serious competition to Cary Grant as the genre's premiere actors. Their on-screen rivalry to impress the wife they (accidentally, of course) share is one of the most overt displays of screwball comedy's couching the romantic pursuits of the economically comfortable in the rowdy but good natured, push-turns-to-shove antics of children. The contrast inherent in Douglas' polished urbanity versus MacMurray's practiced inanity not only heightens the humor, but also displays the range of personality types which the screwball vision could comfortably accommodate.

MacMurray's final screwball showcase came in the same year that most of the other recurrent participants bowed out of the cycle, 1942. *Take a Letter, Darling* cast him as a male secretary to Rosalind Russell's high powered lady boss. The actor's accomplished ability to register alternate moods of comic frustration, warm insincerity, and blundering determination served him very well in what was his seventh collaboration with director Mitchell Leisen. The comic twist in the film is the character's discomfort at sex role reversal, coupled with the effects of his seeming disinterest in his attractive employer.

As was the case with a number of other stars whose prewar forté was in the various forms of romantic comedy, MacMurray successfully extended his career well into the 1950s by accepting an increasing number of roles in serious drama. The closest he ever came to the world of screwball in his subsequent years on screen was in *Murder, He Says* (1945), but its peculiar air of social anarchy was thoroughly suffused with Hillbilly humor and mordant farce. In the 1960s his career was thoroughly rejuvenated with a successful concentration on juvenile comedy (in several Disney films) and domestic humor (via his long-running television series).[8]

Jean Arthur had acted in films since the early 1920s, when she was still a teenager, but a long string of undistinguished and interchangeable ingenue parts caused her to desert Hollywood for Broadway in 1931. This was despite the fact that she had survived the transition to talkies, and it was a career change in direct opposition to the common show business trend of the time—that of moving from stage to screen. Such a contrary approach to entertainment custom was actually typical of this unique performer, who made a lifelong practice of rejecting the glamorous and extroverted behavior expected of a "star" and who gained screen immortality as the personification of the ordinary American working girl.

Arthur's return to Hollywood two years later was greeted, after a couple of freelance jobs, with a Columbia contract. Few accolades were given the studio's shaky attempt to star their new, now stage-trained leading lady in a bald-faced imitation of Helen Hayes' Oscar-win, *The Sin of Madelon Claudet* (1932). The Columbia copy came out under the title *The Most Precious Thing in Life* (1934), with Arthur's character growing from vibrant youth to wizened old age as she secretly sacrifices all for the benefit of the son who will never know his mother. Instead, the performance which catapulted the actress to public prominence was her one-of-the-guys bank clerk who befriends and inspires the timid hero of *The Whole Town's Talking* (1935), an early classic of the screwball genre.

Arthur was perfectly cast as an appealing, supportive, and non-threatening source of sanity amidst the chaotic narrative of mistaken identity, kidnapping, and impersonation. Although her part was by no means screwy, her engagingly confident response to and mastery of the cascade of wild situations made her an ideal point of comic reference. Arthur received more conventional roles in her next few pictures but one of them, *If You Could Only Cook* (1935), veered close enough to screwball in its depiction of a tycoon pretending to be a chef that the studio deceptively spread the word that it was really a Frank Capra picture in the spirit of *It Happened One Night.* The outraged director of that film not only labored to set the public record straight, but he also used Arthur in his authentic next picture, *Mr. Deeds Goes to Town* (1936). Her alternately cynical and sentimental performance in *Deeds*, as the reporter who inspires the title character to become an American folk hero, won her legions of adoring new fans who saw in Arthur the archetypal image of the self-sufficient, working class heroine of the Depression era.

While the Capra film was in essence a populist fable told with aspects of the screwball style, Arthur's subsequent picture, a loan-out assignment at RKO directed by the talented but now forgotten Stephen Roberts, was an apolitical genre hybrid. *The Ex-Mrs. Bradford* (1936) took the screwball approach to crime detection in a zany variant on MGM's *Thin Man* formula, so obvious in its intent that it also had William Powell as its dapper male lead. Here Arthur was given the chance to play a genuine eccentric, a thrill-seeking mystery author who cajoles her former spouse into lending his medical expertise to her attempted solving of a murder. Arthur tackled the role with apparent glee and delivered one of her best and funniest performances. She even topped it at Paramount in 1937, when *Easy Living* presented her as a timid magazine writer whose honest attempt to return a found mink coat to its millionaire owner launches an avalanche of misunderstandings which propel her into a new life of luxury. Under the sensitive guidance of director Mitchell Leisen, Arthur's display of a mixed sense of wonder, vulnerability, and non-threatening sarcasm (despite the aggressively barbed Preston Sturges screenplay) made her character just the sort of modern-day Cinderella with whom the audience could identify, unhindered by even a trace of envy.

When Capra called on her for his second full-fledged screwball project, *You Can't Take It with You* (1938), she was once again cast as the reassuring figure of feminine sanity in the vortex of a whirlwind of benign crazies. Although Arthur was outstanding opposite Cary Grant in *Only Angels Have Wings* (1939), directed by screwball comedy co-founder Howard Hawks, he was just coming off the boxoffice disaster of *Bringing Up Baby* (1938) and *Angels* was instead a poetic airborne adventure of courage and cowardice. Arthur's role called for a careful blend of stoicism, cynicism, and romanticism. Her expanding range as an actress made her equal to the task, but comedy was still her specialty.

Screwball co-founder Capra then had Arthur, in effect, repeat her reporter/counsellor/heroine role from *Mr. Deeds* in *Mr. Smith Goes to Washington* (1939). The filmmaker's newest populist tract in screwball wrapping was hugely successful and firmly assured Arthur's high ranking on the popularity charts. Her next picture was thoroughly screwball, as well as one of the marriage versus remarriage comedies inspired by Irene Dunne's heralded performance in *The Awful Truth* (1937). *Too Many Husbands* (1940) gave Arthur just the right amount of emotional room to flirt with and fend off the attentions of the two previously inattentive spouses her character had sequentially married, believing the first to be deceased until his surprise return.

By this point in her career Arthur was a consummate screen comedienne, knowing exactly how to modulate her impish good humor, to pinch her dryly compassionate voice into only the most appropriate squeaks, and to feign innocently the need of male assistance while sharing with the audience an awareness of her wellspring of spunky self-assurance. Arthur's final screwball performance came as an archetypal shopgirl who humanizes her incognito employer in the Norman Krasna scripted *The Devil and Miss Jones* (1941). Her well intentioned mentoring of what she thinks is an inexperienced but older coworker keenly exemplifies how screwball comedy at its subversive best could diffuse the didacticism of class struggle depiction in an entertainment framework which consistently foregrounds its humor and romance elements, something which Capra, for all his genius as a showman, did only once in his three pictures with Arthur.

Arthur's subsequent pair of pictures for director George Stevens are, by the standards of this study, socially conscious romantic comedies without the frenzy or bite of screwball, but her knowing approach to her characterizations in *The Talk of the Town* (1942) and *The More the Merrier* (1943) still reveal her at the peak of her form. Barely a year later, at the expiration of her Columbia contract, Arthur emphatically announced her retirement from the screen. And except for a couple of one-picture comebacks, she kept her word— preferring to earn a late college degree, fitfully return to the stage, try a television series, and teach drama at Vassar. During her years of stardom, Arthur's offscreen reputation was that of an overly shy performer who shunned extra publicity and had to be coaxed gently into the exuberancce of her characters. At her screwball best some of that shyness is still evident. When she is viewed in contrast with the other major performers in the genre she does stand out as the tamest and sanest of the screwball stars, never really "going wild" but genuinely amused by those around her who do.[9]

MAJOR WRITERS

Hollywood's film studios converted to "all-talking" picture production during the last months of 1920s prosperity, well before the Wall Street crash and the ensuing depression. Experienced writers of fiction were already being lured to the film colony in the last years of silence, but the talkie boom which lay around the corner was fated to increase the migration from the literary bastions on the Hudson several times over. In anticipation of the good times to come, author Herman Mankiewicz dashed off his now-legendary 1926 telegram to ex-journalist and Broadway playwright Ben Hecht:

> Will you accept three hundred per week to work for Paramount Pictures? All expenses paid. Three hundred is peanuts. Millions are to be grabbed out here and your only competition is idiots. Don't let this get around.[10]

Hecht eagerly accepted his friend's characteristically sarcastic invitation, but the word did get around. Spurred on by the successful arrival of dialogue-dependent talking pictures the following year, a host of other professional writers, including novelists, essayists, playwrights and reporters, also boarded trains for the west. Soon they too were busily at work pounding out scripts for the insatiable appetite of the Hollywood entertainment machine. Those writers with journalistic experience often carried over their tabloid sensibilities into finished scripts noted for their acerbic, punchy dialogue and unsentimental, iconoclastic story lines, especially in fictional depictions of the urban lifestyles upon which these scribes had once reported factually.[11]

In like manner the transplanted book, magazine, and stage

authors infused their new film assignments with the polished wit, sophistication, and elegance which had been the hallmarks of their eastern experience. When the cycle of screwball comedy films began a few years later, it would benefit greatly from these New York strains of influence, often filtered through the sight-gag sensibilities of veteran Hollywood directors who had previously excelled in silent comedy. Thus the reporter's wisecrack and the comedian's pratfall entered the drawing rooms of Park Avenue, as recreated on the sound stages of California.

The most celebrated reporter-turned-screenwriter was Ben Hecht, credited with work on more than 50 motion picture scripts, including the outstanding screwball comedies *Twentieth Century* and *Nothing Sacred,* which bitingly satirize the Broadway stage and the newsprint page, respectively. The title of the latter appears to sum up the prolific Hecht's attitude toward American society and its customs, as well as the outlook of screwball comedy in general.

During his long career Hecht wrote in virtually all popular genres, beginning his playwriting career in collaboration with Kenneth Sawyer Goodman on a series of one-act dramas which date from 1914. Hecht's first full-length play, "The Egotist," was, like his later *Twentieth Century,* about a tyrannical stage producer. It had a New York opening in 1922, but its Chicago based writer did not relocate to the theater capital until two years later. At that time his departure was mourned on the front page of a rival paper as a serious loss for the Windy City, where he had supplemented his newspaper work by writing novels and publishing an ambitious magazine called the *Chicago Literary Times.* Hecht had also gained notoriety as something of a Dadaist and as a defendant in a federal obscenity case.[12]

Ben Hecht's name regularly appears as co-author in the long list of his works, and he clearly enjoyed engaging in literary collaboration. In New York he began his long-time partnership with another ex–Chicago reporter, Charles MacArthur. Although they had worked for rival papers, their common memories of covering crime stories and the courthouse beat served them exceedingly well in crafting their satirical farce about ruthless reporters and corrupt politicians, "The Front Page." It opened on Broadway in 1928 for a successful run of 281 performances.

Despite Hecht's eager acceptance of ex-reporter Herman Mankiewicz' invitation to easy money in Hollywood (where Hecht's debut screenplay for *Underworld* earned him a $10,000 bonus for only a few days' work) he resisted the temptation to "go Hollywood" on a permanent basis, as so many other stage and printed-page authors did. Commanding the industry's top price for scripts in the 1930s ($50,000 to $100,000 each) Hecht lived half of each year at his Eastern home in Nyack, New York. He appears to have suffered little from the legendary bitterness which gripped so many Gotham authors who came to feel that their Hollywood years ultimately resulted in a prostituting of their literary talents. Hecht regarded screenwriting as an "amiable chore," despite the inevitable distortions imposed by directors, producers, and teams of re-write authors. Hecht himself was viewed as a reliable "script doctor," who was often brought in (sometimes uncredited) to repair a shaky script after the manner of Broadway's eminent "Mr. Fix-it," George S. Kaufman. Hecht willingly accepted all kinds of writing assignments, even hack ones, and cynically admitted that it took no less energy doing good work: "It's just as hard to make a toilet seat as it is a castle window. But the view is different."[13]

Hecht's expertise at story construction, character delineation, and narrative pacing served him well in writing for all sorts of movies, but it is his early defining of the screwball style in *Twentieth Century*, his vitriolic summation of it in *Nothing Sacred*, his indirect contributions to its revisionist masterpiece *His Girl Friday*, and his anarchic postscript to the cycle, *Monkey Business*, which are of prime importance to this study.

Another significant screenwriter in the history of screwball comedy, Norman Krasna, also came from the ranks of the New York newspaper world. Working his way up from copyboy to become drama editor and critic of the *New York Evening Graphic* by 1929, Krasna branched out into the film business the following year as a columnist for the trade paper *Exhibitor's Herald-World*. This position, in turn, led to a $50-a-week job in Hollywood in the Warner Brothers publicity department. Ben Hecht's rise to success had so inspired Krasna that while still in New York, he had practiced the craft of playwriting by means of repeatedly typing the script of "The Front Page" in order to study its construction. Just as Hecht and MacArthur had based their smash on first-hand experience in a dingy Chicago press room, Krasna composed a stage play on the basis of the excesses he had observed and participated in as a studio public relations man. The result was titled "Louder, Please," a frenetic 1931 satire of a studio press agent (played by Lee Tracy, star of "The Front Page") who stages an actress' (Louise Brooks) phony disappearance at sea in order to generate some ink and attention. Although the play ran for only 68 performances on Broadway, its bright dialogue convinced Columbia Pictures to put Krasna under contract as a screenwriter. Like Hecht, Krasna worked on stories from various genres and moved from one studio to another, coming to specialize in warm, romantic comedy-dramas while continuing to write for the stage as well.[14] In 1935 at Paramount, he had, in collaboration, his first hit in something resembling the screwball vein, *Hands Across the Table*. It featured the first starring role specially tailored for the actress who was to personify the spirit of such films, Carole Lombard, as a manicurist hunting a rich husband. Other Krasna films displaying screwball elements included *Wife Versus Secretary* (1936), *The King and the Chorus Girl* (1937), and *Bachelor Mother* (1939), but it was not until 1941, with *Mr. and Mrs. Smith,* that he embraced the by-then fully established formula in the extreme, and again it was for the benefit of its definitive screwball star, Carole Lombard, who this time started out the story happily married, only to discover that her marriage was not legal.

Krasna immediately followed up that same year with another screwball classic, *The Devil and Miss Jones,* pitting an archetypal shopgirl (Jean Arthur), against her disguised boss, with a not quite so comic background of labor unrest. Krasna garnered an Oscar nomination for his screenplay, which was based once again on personal experience years earlier, while working under difficult conditions in a department store. The balance of Krasna's career, which included producing as well as writing for other stage and screen, saw him specializing in more mainstream romantic comedy again, frequently employing his characteristic mistaken identity plots, tinged with mild criticism of social injustice. "Comedy," Krasna said, "gives me more chances to do the kinds of statements I want to make."[15]

Robert Riskin, another celebrated comedy screenwriter, would certainly have agreed with that observation. Several of the films to which Riskin contributed go far beyond the generally apolitical, cynic's eye view of American society associated with screwball comedy. In fact their clearly populist sentiments, championing society's "little people" against the "big bosses," so upstage the screwball antics which surround them that a clear controversy has arisen among film historians as to whether any of Riskin's films actually merit the pure appellation of screwball comedy—or instead deserve to be categorized separately.[16]

Riskin was yet another Broadway playwright of the 1920s who followed up on selling his plays ("Illicit," "Many a Slip") to the talkies by moving to Hollywood and writing fresh material directly for the screen. Already experienced in collaborating with co-authors, Riskin adapted well to the multiple author system of the film studios and continued to work as a screenwriter for the next 20 years. During that time it was his frequent collaborations with director Frank Capra which earned him the highest recognition. The relationship began in 1931 with Capra's following up on directing a film version (*Miracle Woman*) of a Riskin play about a faith healer ("Bless You Sister") by employing Riskin to write dialogue for *Platinum Blonde,* the story of a working-class reporter whose better instincts are stifled by a mismatched marriage to a wealthy society girl. Ultimately the movie's situation is righted by the writer's romantic return to his true element, now in the company of a more equal and inspiring mate—a girl reporter he had foolishly overlooked before.

The Riskin-Capra comedic crusade for class consciousness and populist justice is much overshadowed by the witty dialogue, star turns and sexual tension of their early proto-screwball triumph, the multi–Oscar-winning *It Happened One Night* (1934), but later efforts such as *Mr. Deeds Goes to Town* and *Meet John Doe* foregrounded their Depression inspired calls to "share the wealth" and "beat the bosses." Riskin's most intensely screwball assignment, the 1938 *You Can't Take It with You,* was actually an adaptation of the Kaufman-Ferber stage hit about an hilariously eccentric extended family of self-expressives whose lack of concern for societal norms makes them vulnerable to capitalist pressures. In comparison it appears that Riskin's version softens the bite of the original work, replacing the masked anger with populist faith that class compromise (symbolized by a harmonica duet) is still possible in a Depression weary America.

Riskin's screwball style gangster satire, *The Whole Town's Talking* (1935), was done not with Capra but with John Ford, and Riskin's Cary Grant/Grace Moore musical comedy, *When You're in Love* (1937), was an early and isolated experiment in placing a veteran screenwriter in the director's chair. Riskin never attempted directing again. He helped round out MGM's long-running series of screwball style mysteries by writing *The Thin Man Goes Home* for a 1944 release, and by the time he had returned (without Capra) to populist subject matter (the corrupting influence of public opinion polls) in *Magic Town* (1947) his vision, interpreted by arch-cynic director William Wellman, seemed to have turned from optimism to gloom. One of Riskin's last projects, Edmund Goulding's *Mr. 880* (1950) resignedly evoked sympathy for a humble old counterfeiter who provides a subsistence pension for himself by cranking out one-dollar bills.

Screwball screenwriter Billy Wilder began as a crime reporter in Austria and Germany, tried his hand at cabaret entertaining, and eventually found regular work writing screenplays in the last years before the Nazi takeover. When he joined the flood of exiles to Hollywood, some of his compatriots employed him on their American projects, including Ernst Lubitsch's 1938 foray into screwball territory, *Bluebeard's Eighth Wife*, in which a much-married millionaire is first chased and later driven crazy by an aggressively daffy gold digger. Wilder's frequent Hollywood collaborator was yet another exile from the eastern literary set, former *New Yorker* drama critic Charles Brackett, whose sense of public taste (including his own) helped to contain the blend of Viennese jaundice and Berliner bile which made up the Wilder approach to sentiment and romance.

Lubitsch called on the pair a second time for 1939's *Ninotchka*, in which "Garbo laughed" amidst an energetic satire on Communist stoicism corrupted by Parisian high life. For ace romantic stylist Mitchell Leisen, Wilder and Brackett crafted that same year the screwball classic *Midnight*, which used the familiar Paramount-Paris setting for an adventure in gold-digging in which an unemployed chorine capers in the salons of the rich in a Cinderella-like role of intentionally mistaken identity.

Wilder and Brackett covered several genres as their successful collaboration grew, but their only other screwball outing was for Howard Hawks' 1941 *Ball of Fire*, in which another fairy tale received a modern send-up. This time it was the story of "Snow White," whom the writers transmogrified into a burlesque stripper on the run not from a wicked queen, but from a gangster chieftain. The dwarves who hide her are diminished not so much in physical stature as in contemporary socialization. They are a group of college professors — sequestered while writing a new encyclopedia.

Wilder's fondness for stories of role-playing carried over into his first American directing assignment, *The Major and the Minor* (1942), in which he exploited the popular response to Ginger Rogers' impersonation of a child in her Oscar-winning role as *Kitty Foyle* (1940), by devising a screwball opportunity for her to play an even younger girl. Her character's ruse (in order to travel by train at reduced fare) is extended through the balance of the story, complicating the sexual tension and cultural clash between the girl and her new surroundings—a boys' military academy—echoing the contrast between the stripper and the professors in *Ball of Fire*.

As the screwball cycle of films came to a close with the altered attitudes of Hollywood in wartime, Wilder and Brackett moved on to more serious dramas. Their considerably later ventures in screen humor would be more aptly described as bordering on "black humor," although in the 1970s Wilder did attempt a remake of Hecht and MacArthur's "The Front Page." The precedent which allowed Wilder to move from being a Paramount staff writer to becoming one of its fledgling directors was set two years earlier when studio contractee Preston Sturges was given a similar promotion. (Since more of his contributions to the screwball cycle were in the capacity of writer-director, he is covered in the directors' chapter of this study.)

One Chicago journalist turned screwball comedy writer came to his later profession not by first switching to the stage or by scaling the literary heights of the *New Yorker*, but by chronicling the foibles and exploits of show business in the trade paper *Variety*. Claude Binyon did manage to get some reviewing assignments during his term with the paper, but it was one of his contributions as a headline writer which earned him a small slice of immortality. His heading for *Variety*'s story on the 1929 stock market crash read: "Wall Street Lays an Egg."

Binyon spent seven years at the trade paper while attempting to start a second career as a magazine writer. His lack of attention to his *Variety* duties cost him his job, but through industry connections he eventually found work as a screen writer.[17] His first credit was for *The Gilded Lily* (1935), a screwball satire of the publicity-hungry show business world he had come to know so well. His insider's view of how a no-talent singer (played by a non-dubbed Claudette Colbert) could be built into a crowd-drawing celebrity was brought to the screen by veteran Paramount director Wesley Ruggles, who was so pleased with Binyon's gift for comedy that the two became a team and worked together regularly for eight years.

The easy-going, portly, and self-effacing Binyon, nicknamed "Buttercake" by his collaborator, specialized in romance and comedy, and his work in those two broad categories crossed over into screwball territory on four other memorable occasions, two of which came in 1937. *I Met Him in Paris* had its heroine (again, Claudette Colbert) romantically and frantically pursued by two suitors on a European skiing vacation; *True Confession* satirized the publicity circus attendant to a false murder confession by a well-meaning scatterbrain (Carole Lombard). A Binyon-Ruggles offering of 1940, *Too Many Husbands*, reworked the familiar "Enoch Arden" theme of a lost-and-found extra spouse for actress Jean Arthur, and Binyon's 1942 screenplay for Mitchell Leisen, *Take a Letter, Darling,* drew laughs from reversing the customary sex roles of boss and secretary (Claudette Colbert and Fred MacMurray).

Binyon continued to write for a variety of other directors, and from 1948–53 served as director of his own screenplays. Towards the end of his career he collaborated on two late projects of screwball comedy veteran Leo McCarey, but the results of *Rally 'Round the Flag, Boys* (1958) and *Satan Never Sleeps* (1962) were very much of another era. Like Herman Mankiewicz before him, Binyon held no inflated impression of his enjoyable work. Writing under the byline of Captain Claude Binyon in *Variety's* 1945 anniversary issue, he took a tongue-in-cheek look at his craft:

> Writing for motion pictures is so simple and the reward is so great, that one wonders why no more than several hundred persons have chosen it over cab-driving as a career. Of course, it is admitted that a cab driver meets more interesting people, but a motion picture writer may work for good pay during the day and pretend to meet interesting people at night.
>
> Everyone knows that in the average picture a boy will meet a girl and they will fall in love, have a dilly of a spat, then become reconciled. Why doesn't everyone write it? Is it simply laziness on their part? The weekly pay ranges from over $100 a week to thousands. Just for that: just for putting on paper about the boy and the girl.[18]

MAJOR DIRECTORS

The first directors of movie comedy, during the earliest years of dramatic narrative in the silent era (1903–1915), frequently needed little more material than a banana peel, a piece of pavement, and an unsuspecting stroller. By experimentation these pioneer laugh-makers learned that the audience response would be greater if the victim of the mishap were, perhaps, fat. Adding a top hat gave him the appearance of power and authority, thus making the laughter and applause greeting his sudden, even violent comeuppance still more intense. This was simple comedy for simple viewers, many of them recent immigrants with little social sophistication or even a working knowledge of English.

Movie comedy makers filled the last years of silence with more complex and carefully structured plot surprises and deflations of pretension, as befitted the arrival of middle-class audiences to the ornate movie palaces which replaced the storefront nickelodeons in the post–WWI era.[19] Silent comedy in the 1920s reached exquisite heights of visual wit and technical brilliance, only to see its seemingly perfected art form swept away by the stampede to sound in 1928–29. The new overemphasis on stage derived dialogue, often delivered in full evening dress by upper-class leading characters whose types had once been only foils for the silent comics, could indeed be witty, but in a literary way which had previously been directed only at the affluent patrons of the Broadway theater. "Drawing room" comedy, as it was called, tried hard to maintain its dignity in all situations, for fine manners and correct deportment were part and parcel of the impression of quality and breeding.

To be sure, there was low verbal comedy too, in the first years of sound, and it thrived even more as audiences thrilled to the supposedly authentic urban accents, slang, and vocal mannerisms of its blue-collar characters, who appeared to take rough pride in their roguishly uninhibited, sometimes rowdy, even uncouth behavior. However, neither high nor low comedy succeeded in mixing well with the other in those first talkie years (1929–33), or in rekindling the creative spark of silent comedy at its best, even though the directors of that legendary screen specialty did, for the most part, continue to work in the industry.

Crediting a breakthrough to one man is always risky business for the cinema historian, but the status of screwball landmark film can be confidently conferred on a 1934 picture directed by silent comedy veteran Frank Capra, who dared to cross genre boundaries, class lines, and audience expectations. His multi–Oscar-winning *It Happened One Night* glorified the common sense of the working man, warmly mocked the sheltered rich, and did so both visually and verbally, escaping the drawing rooms of the mansion to roam rural America on a cross-country bus trip with the common people. Based on a *Cosmopolitan* magazine short story about a rich girl's reluctant romance with a working man, the project had numerous false starts and setbacks, causing its near-cancellation before the shooting had even begun. The literature of Hollywood is filled with various accounts of how the borrowed leading players, Clark Gable from MGM and Claudette Colbert from Paramount, saw their assignment to a cheap Columbia picture as no more than drudgery, while studio boss Harry Cohn nearly pulled the plug on the project because of the story's unpromising similarity to a minor cycle of romantic dramas set on board public transportation.[20] Yet the finished film went on to score a then-record of five top Academy Awards, including Best Picture, and established key elements of what would later be called the screwball style. *It Happened One Night*'s staggering success made it ripe for imitation, and the major studios' race was soon on to identify and copy (with other stars and stories) what were suspected to be the winning components in the Capra-Riskin comedic recipe.

Several other tales of runaway heiresses ultimately reached the screen, but none matched the public approval given their inspiration. A wider and more lasting influence of Capra's fashioning of the film lay in how the picture depicted the lives of the rich, contrasting their often petty motivations and silly behavior with the down-to-earth, common sense of the working class, but at the same time displaying a genuine sympathy for the wealthy, viewing them as so isolated from the realities of the lunchbox and paycheck world that they retained a serious degree of childish naïveté well into their adult years. In light of the political/economic realities of 1933–34, with the New Deal struggling to build a national consensus out of the possibly revolutionary chaos of financial collapse, Capra's film supplied a calming fantasy—that the rich were not public enemies after all, only misunderstood, spoiled children, and that their misbehavior could be great fun to watch.

Capra's experience as a writer and director of silent comedies for Hal Roach and Mack Sennett, culminating in the creation of Harry Langdon's best films and unique screen image, had given Capra a masterful command of the tricks and technology of film storytelling, but his first work in the sound era concentrated on heroic rescue-adventure and conventional melodrama, not comedy. It was his subsequent partnering with screenwriter Robert Riskin that led Capra to confront and exploit class difference and conflict as his dramas' driving force. Fine as the team's work was on such films as *American Madness, Platinum Blonde* (both 1931), *Broadway Bill*, and *Lady for a Day* (both 1933), it was only the unexpected triumph of *It Happened One Night* that extended the Capra-Riskin influence across both the 1930s film industry and its subsequent history.

Capra worked closely with Riskin, scene by scene with the latter usually composing the dialogue and the former guiding the narrative structure and editing the copy. On the set Capra made full use of his extraordinary technical skill, most notably in speeding up the delivery of lines and pacing of action by roughly 40 percent without making the results appear forced or unnatural. While shooting *It Happened One Night*, however, the production team's shared suspicion that the picture was going to fail led to a looseness of approach, much joking on the set, and even ad-libbing through several scenes.[21] When wild, unheard of for Columbia, success greeted the result, this carefree approach to movie making became a key ingredient of the screwball cycle which followed.

As sometimes happens where artistic innovation is concerned, the authors quickly moved on to other matters of more pressing personal concern (such as the political trilogy of *Mr. Deeds Goes to Town, Mr. Smith Goes to Washington,* and *Meet John Doe*), leaving the field clear for others to pick up on the nascent screwball trend and turn it into a viable phenomenon to which many varied and talented filmmakers would contribute before it had run its course. Even Capra's most overtly screwball picture, released in 1938 when the cycle was in full swing (*You Can't Take It with You*) carries a socio-political message which overshadows the anarchic romp through screwball territory. Capra's wartime production of *Arsenic and Old Lace*, a very close filming of a rapid fire Broadway farce about elderly, insane mercy killers, has the sound and fury of screwball, but not the content. His last directorial assignments, ranging from Christmas fantasy and political exposé to science documentaries and star vehicles for pop vocalists, while sometimes rising to screwball heights of enthusiasm, were all postwar in the most pro-social sense and devoid of screwball's pesky but pleasing obeisance to anarchy.

Yet the question of Frank Capra's status as a screwball comedy director remains a point of controversy among film historians, since their definitions in some cases do allow for inclusion of a wide body of 1930s screen comedy under the screwball heading, regardless of how a film treats money and politics, as long as the picture is fast-paced and employs witty antagonism to develop romantic relationships, whether or not they cross class boundaries.[22] Capra, as his films so emphatically demonstrate, came to take the power and misuse of wealth very seriously. The wealthy, weary, and good-natured father of *It Happened One Night* is a far cry from the malevolent millionaires who menace both the lovers and society in general in subsequent Capra pictures, wherein the populist cry for solidarity among the masses is quite out of harmony with the escapist ethic of pure screwball, which painted the powerful as benignly silly and more deserving of our amused pity than our wary concern.

To say that Howard Hawks made some of the very best screwball comedies is to state both the obvious and to commit serious understatement, for Hawks has been lauded by critics and historians as a master of many genres.[23] Due in part to his uncanny choice of expert collaborators, he managed during his long career to create outstanding works in western, gangster, musical, adventure, and detective cinema, in addition to his definitive contributions to screwball comedy. Hawks began in movies as a prop man, later worked as an editor and writer, and moved into directing films in the mid-1920s. His experience in silent comedy, with such films as *Fig Leaves* and *Cradle Snatchers*, served him well after the changeover to sound, for it was in the crucial year of 1934 that he directed one of the key films which helped to define the screwball style.

Twentieth Century shared more in common with *It Happened One Night* (also 1934) than a cross-country, public transportation setting. It was also influential, albeit for different reasons, in setting standards to which subsequent screwball directors and their films would aspire. The dialogue is not only delivered at a rapid pace, but the characters overlap the end of one speech with the beginning of the next, appearing to interrupt each other as in an ad-libbed encounter. Wisecracks and insults pepper the conversations, as the rich and beautiful leading players, in this case a top Broadway producer and his glamorous leading lady, spend a long-distance train trip arguing the sticking points in their stormy but hugely successful, interlocking careers. The source material, a stage play by Ben Hecht and Charles MacArthur, is indicative of screwball comedy's clear indebtedness to the sophisticated barbs of Broadway dialogue-fests, but it was Hawks' deft staging and pacing, combined with his inspired casting, which created a hit movie which other Hollywood hands then sought to imitate in style and attitude. The driving ambition and deviousness visible in John Barrymore's verbally florid portrayal of stage "genius" Oscar Jaffe give the proceedings a continuing air of barely controlled dementia, with his shrieks of hyperbole and invective matched and sometimes bested by Carole Lombard's near hysterical and sharp-tongued retorts — in the role of temperamental star Lilly Garland, an unwilling and often frantic Trilby to his megalomaniacal, Manhattan Svengali.

Just as Frank Capra started things rolling, quickly moved on to projects of another sort, then a few years later revisited the genre he had cofounded, Hawks busied himself with films from other genres until 1938, when he went screwball a second time and came up with what is widely regarded as one of the cycle's two or three best examples. *Bringing Up Baby* employed the sexual antagonism masking attraction game of *Twentieth Century* from a different angle, with a willful, madcap rich girl (considerably more unpredictable than the heiress of *It Happened One Night*) romantically pursuing a timid professor of paleontology, who in turn is pursuing a missing dinosaur bone, a playful terrier, and the eccentric young lady's pet leopard. The breathtaking pace of the continually funny dialogue, delivered quite seriously by the highly attractive players (Cary Grant and Katharine Hepburn), coupled with a spiraling plot-web of improbable complications and embarrassments, may have been too extreme for the contemporary audience, already surfeited by a barrage of screwball predecessors on their screens, for the film was unsuccessful during its first release and gained its high critical and popular approval years later via retrospective screenings, which revealed its saturated perfection in rendering the screwball vision.

Hawks' adventure dramas reveled in worshipful depictions of

courageous groups of men who undertook dangerous jobs with sobriety, professionalism, and supreme devotion to duty. His forays into screwball territory retained a sense of such genuine devotion by the main characters, but the gravity of their commitment quickly dissolved in panic and frivolity, awash in the improbable consequences of their efforts. *Ball of Fire* (1941) portrayed another bookish professor, again played against type, this time by stalwart Gary Cooper, in a sequestered quest to write a new dictionary with the collaboration of a group of older and individually eccentric academics. Into their ultra-serious state of seclusion bursts not a high-spirited heiress, but a fugitive (from the mob) burlesque queen, and the clash of cultures, enhanced by physical danger and enlivened by her wisecracks and overt eroticism, swirls the ingredients of the screwball stew.

Hawks' final comedy offerings reached the screen well after the screwball cycle had ended, but they both starred the actor who had become, following his initiation in *Bringing Up Baby*, the epitome of the screwball leading man. In *I Was a Male War Bride*, more pointedly titled in Britain as *You Can't Sleep Here* (1949), the sexual tension crosses national cultures rather than social classes, as Grant most improbably portrays a French army officer whose marrriage to an American WAC (Ann Sheridan) results in a frantic and complex series of mishaps which repeatedly require him to dress in female attire and postpone their wedding night. Apart from Hawks' characteristic pacing and style of line delivery, it is the contrived and merciless humiliation of the male romantic lead, either by the assertive heroine or by circumstance, which provides the connecting link between this postwar bedroom farce and the prewar screwball cycle. Gone are the penthouses, private cars, Manhattan night spots, and country homes of the rich. Instead what Hawks creates is a screwball reminiscent drag act, powered by the most explicit form of sexual frustration the censors of the day would permit. Latter-day critical readings of both the Hawksian world of maleness and the alleged inverse relationship of Grant's screen and personal identity give this film a complexity of textual meanings which set it even more apart from the screwball mainstream of this study.

In *Monkey Business* (1952) Hawks resurrected another theme of the original screwball cycle, the reversion to childish behavior by supposedly sophisticated adults, and foregrounded this single idea for the duration of the picture. Once more Cary Grant played a professor, this time a scientist whose youth serum, in the wrong hands,

causes personal chaos for his circle of intimates and raucous amusement for the viewer. The late entries in Hawks' adventure film series
followed, until finally, in 1964, he directed a full-blown tribute to the
cycle he had helped to initiate. *Man's Favorite Sport* was centered
around a curious reworking of a familiar situation from classic screwball comedy—the aggressive, pursuing female vs. the timid, bookish
male. In the key humiliation scene (re-created not from his own
works but from the 1936 *Libeled Lady*) the author of a popular book
on fishing (a part intended for the seemingly ageless Cary Grant but
given to, of all people, Rock Hudson) is forced to demonstrate his
prowess with rod and reel. The aquatic catastrophes which ensue are
squarely in the anarchic spirit with which screwball began, 30 years
earlier.

Although he is not credited with giving the genre a breakthrough film to equal the early contributions of Capra and Hawks,
silent comedy veteran Leo McCarey proved to be far more consistent
in making the screwball vision his own. In the 1920s it was he, more
so than the other Hal Roach directors with whom they worked, who
guided the development of Laurel and Hardy's screen characters.
McCarey's gift for comedy crossed the sound barrier with ease, and
he went on to distinguish himself by obtaining superb performances
from some of the greatest character comedians of the time: Eddie
Cantor, W.C. Fields, Mae West, Burns and Allen, and the Marx
Brothers. McCarey became famous for his propensity to encourage
ad-libbing from cast members, who were already charmed by the
conviviality he established on the set. The sense of happy performers
having slightly giddy fun pervades a great deal of McCarey's work,
and by the time of his 1935 *Ruggles of Red Gap*, a western-set
screwball tale of an English butler's interaction with the American
frontier and the newly rich family he serves, McCarey had reached
the threshold of succession to Ernst Lubitsch (whose forte was sly,
continental humor) as Hollywood's comedy king (allowing for the
parallel supremacy of Frank Capra in using film humor to support the
political ideology of the New Deal).

McCarey cinched the unofficial title with *The Awful Truth*, his
1937 screwball reworking of a 1922 stage play about a divorcing couple who rediscover their love on the eve of their final decree. As
played by the debonair Cary Grant and the radiant Irene Dunne, the
pair gleefully give vent to their most mischievous urges (to spoil each
other's remarriage plans) while indulging in the pleasures of the
penthouse and nightclub fantasy world which befit their well-to-

do status. McCarey even mixed in a touch of screwball fun with the teary-eyed sentiment of his romantic comedy masterpiece, *Love Affair* (1939), which featured another endearing performance by Irene Dunne, this time paired with the ideally cast Charles Boyer as an international playboy/cad, redeemed by the love of a kept but not caught businesswoman turned cabaret singer.

A car crash prevented the accident-prone McCarey from actually directing his hilarious reversal of the famous "Enoch Arden" story, *My Favorite Wife* (1940). McCarey did, however, work on the script, serve as producer, and carefully guide the credited director, Garson Kanin, through the story of a lost-at-sea wife (Irene Dunne) who returns home seven years later and ponders the alternatives of renewed marriage to her original husband (Cary Grant) or legal union with the virile "Adam" (Randolph Scott) to whom she played "Eve" while marooned on a desert island for seven years.[24]

McCarey's *Once Upon a Honeymoon* (1942) tackled the difficult task of mixing a screwball outlook with early wartime propaganda, in a story of the growing attraction between a U.S. government agent (Cary Grant) and an important Nazi's wife (Ginger Rogers) who accompanies her husband on an ocean voyage immediately following their ill-advised marriage. As the screwball cycle faded, McCarey turned to a new sub-genre of his own creation, sentimental religious comedy (*Going My Way*, 1944; *The Bells of St. Mary's*, 1945), and did not even attempt to revive the screwball approach until the late 1950s. His remake of *Love Affair*, called *An Affair to Remember* (1957) gave Cary Grant a chance to shine in the old Charles Boyer role, but refined Deborah Kerr, in the Irene Dunne part, gave little indication her character had once been a semi-screwball type. To the director's credit, however, the sentiment still worked very well, and a four-hanky cry was enjoyed by many viewers. In *Rally 'Round the Flag, Boys!* (1958) McCarey did try valiantly to give a screwball spin to a Broadway derived, cold war comedy about nuclear missiles, but the result was much more topical than tipsy.

McCarey was highly praised during his ultimately uneven career for his exceptionally sensitive powers of observation regarding human motivation and behavior. Until the early 1950s, when his anti-communist family tragedy *My Son John* (1952) made him a pariah among Hollywood liberals, he was very well liked throughout the industry, and his comedy sense was thought by many to have no equal. McCarey's contributions to the screwball cycle are particularly memorable for their finely drawn characterizations, which avoid broad caricature (though such excesses in others' films do add to the merriment) in favor of seemingly real people—caught up in the sometimes improvised antics of chasing each other, in snappy dinner attire, across a fantasy big-town landscape of sleek limousines, chic night spots, mid-town mansions, and art-deco, penthouse apartments, staffed with wryly amused servants.[25]

The fourth in our cadre of master directors of screwball comedy is still another veteran of silent laugh-making, the ex-cartoonist who softened W.C. Fields' rough edges for the screen, Gregory La Cava. Like McCarey, he was a very heavy social drinker, and for a time his alcohol-fueled joviality seemed to fit in well with the liberating buoyancy of his best films. Eventually, however, this shared addiction took its painful toll, and the work of both men suffered a premature decline.

La Cava had moved into directing live-action films in the early 1920s, after turning out animated versions of newspaper cartoons syndicated by the Hearst press, including the absurdly violent "Krazy Kat" and the domestically turbulent "Katzenjammer Kids." Motifs from this very popular material turned up in his silent features, most notably with Ziegfeld star W.C. Fields (*So's Your Old Man*, 1926); *Running Wild*, 1927), whom La Cava cast as an archetypal henpecked husband and father. Like Hawks and McCarey, La Cava was frequently a writer and independent producer on his films, enabling him to impose a strong personal view on the material, moving from one studio to another in search of the kind of independence hard to achieve in the Hollywood of his day.

La Cava's move from cartooning to silent comedy was quite successful, starting with low-budget, Johnny Hines comedies and moving on to some of Richard Dix' best star vehicles for Paramount, including the delightful pair *Womanhandled* (1925) and *Let's Get Married* (1926). While working at Pathé with the young Carole Lombard, the studio was absorbed into the newly formed RKO, and La Cava quickly became one of its major directors. Teamed with the fast-talking Lee Tracy in *The Half-Naked Truth* (1932) La Cava proved himself a master of the rapid-fire, verbal combat tradition of comedy which would soon become, along with visual slapstick, an important ingredient of the screwball style. His 1934 *Affairs of Cellini*, a costume romance about the historic Italian silversmith, was also a pseudo–Renaissance bedroom farce, as screwball in sentiment as his later, modern dress entries in the genre would be.

By this point in La Cava's life he had undergone psychoanalysis and had become a convert to Freudian concepts, which he took to the screen for Paramount the next year in *Private Worlds,* a mental-hospital drama costarring Claudette Colbert. In the wake of the success of Colbert's previous Columbia project, *It Happened One Night,* that studio was anxious to have her try something similar the next time they obtained her services. The deal which made it possible called for the freelancing La Cava to direct Colbert in *She Married Her Boss* (1935), certainly a case of the title telling all. The Freudian underpinning is unmistakable in the story of a stern, inhibited businessman/widower whose personal life is transformed by the liberating ministrations of his extroverted, fun-loving secretary. The style and sensibility of such a sugar-coated prescription fitted in well with the rising screwball cycle.

La Cava's next package deal, with himself as producer, was sold to Universal and allowed him to re-unite with an old friend from their Pathé days, Carole Lombard, who by 1936 was also freelancing and moving away from the serious dramas in which she had slowly risen to middle-rank stardom. Several of La Cava's earlier works had demonstrated his interest in the personality changes wrought by wealth, or the lack of it, and his 1936 *My Man Godfrey* zeroed in on the issue with considerable comic insight. The tale of a spoiled debutante, her selfish and silly family, and the worldly-wise butler (recruited from the city dump) who shows them the error of their ways became an enormous and influential hit. As a result, Lombard's ongoing screen character was re-defined in terms of zaniness, La Cava redoubled his high reputation as a comedy craftsman, and the term "screwball" was first applied by a reviewer to a film. And thus this baseball expression was transformed into a means of grasping and identifying the contemporary trend in boisterous, high-class mischief that had been building on the screen since the arrival of the New Deal and the tightening of the movie censorship code. The appellation stuck, so to speak, and both the public and the industry at last had a handle on the new and accelerating comedy cycle.

La Cava then directed three pictures for his former home studio, RKO, and each, despite their differing genres, settings and sources, displayed some aspects of the screwball style. *Stage Door* (1937), from the Kaufman-Ferber Broadway success about a group of aspiring actresses (including Ginger Rogers) versus the theatrical establishment, was extensively altered by La Cava, but the tragi-comic results still did well with the public and critics. *Fifth Avenue Girl* (1939) reworked the now authentically screwball *Godfrey* premise at a lower decibel level, with a destitute waif (Ginger Rogers) being "adopted" by a dispirited tycoon because his spoiled family brings him only grief. *Primrose Path* (1940), the most serious of the trio, veered from comedy into melodrama as it tackled a seemingly impossible project—dodging the censors in refilming an old property the studio owned about a whore's daughter (again, Ginger Rogers) trying to make good.

It was not until fairly late in the screwball cycle, 1941, that La Cava returned to the studio of his triumph in the genre, Universal, but it did offer him two treasured opportunities to work with another of the great screwball stars, Irene Dunne. (His only previous picture with Dunne had been 1932's Jewish ghetto drama, *Symphony of Six Million*, before her remarkable changeover to comedy.) *Unfinished Business* riskily mixed simplified Freud and screwball fun in portraying a romance imperiled by the Dunne character's nagging memories of a previous affair with her new love interest's brother. The waning of the screwball cycle seemed to be acknowledged by La Cava in his unsuccessful follow-up, *Lady in a Jam* (1942), in which Dunne's character is treated by a psychiatrist who tries to cure her of being— such a screwball!

La Cava completed no films during the next five years, and his comeback (and final film) was a rather modest, Gene Kelly semi-musical about a returning WWII serviceman, *Living in a Big Way* (1947). Despite its song-and-dance conventions, the picture was far removed from the pretend world of pre-war screwball and was genuinely concerned with the attractions and difficulties of middle-class, domestic life.[25]

Our last major director of screwball comedy sat out the 1930s in the writer's chair, not gaining studio authorization to direct one of his own scripts until just before the turn of the decade. Preston Sturges did, however, make a major contribution to the genre at its height—by authoring the screenplay of *Easy Living* (1937), the story of a shopgirl whose accidental retrieval of a millionaire's discarded mink coat sets off a chain of events in which suspicions of her being his mistress lead her to the good fortune of marrying his son. Like *Bringing Up Baby*, *Easy Living* was not widely recognized as an all-time screwball classic until well after the cycle had ended.

Although he had specialized in dialogue-rich, romantic comedy since his early career as a Broadway playwright, of the 15 other films Sturges worked on during his first ten years in movies only *Thirty Day Princess* (1934), a satire on publicity stunts and *Hotel Haywire*

(1937), a dizzying farce about a crooked astrologer, could be said to contain any of the elements of screwball comedy in their finished versions. It was not until Sturges finally convinced the Paramount executives to let him direct, that his expertise in employing the screwball outlook became fully apparent. He had been a devoted student of other people's movies since the 1920s, taking notes on whatever aspects of a film impressed him and worked well with an audience. Once in a publicity article he even set down a list of the most effective plot devices regularly exploited by Hollywood to please the customers. When Sturges began directing he not only made liberal use of such events in his stories, but did so in the self-satirical style of a movie insider, following a consistent policy of casting his secondary roles almost exclusively with a select group of eccentric character actors whose work he had admired in 1930s comedies. This cadre of performers soon came to be known as the "Sturges stock company."[26]

Sturges' first films as director were actually updatings of original, unsold scripts he had written several years earlier, when the screwball cycle was just beginning. His directorial debut, *The Great McGinty* (1940), was a political satire of how a bum's first successful job in politics, voting early and often for pay, leads to his rise to power in the party and eventual corrupt success as governor of the "mythical" state of Illinois. The man's swift downfall (in keeping with the famous saloon song, "Down Went McGinty," which was also the screenplay's original title) comes as the result of his first honest act while serving as a figurehead/stooge for the political "machine." That same year Sturges also brought to the screen *Christmas in July*, another of his unfilmed, early-1930s projects, previously titled "A Cup of Coffee." Sturges' penchant for satire was directed this time at radio slogan contests, in a story of a lowly clerk tricked into believing he has won a fortune in consumer-goods prizes. Both low budgeted films were as fast paced and as filled with verbal fireworks and doses of slapstick as the best of the screwball cycle which preceded them to the screen, but their topically satirical aspects did set them apart from the more general, fun-and-games pursuits of romance and pleasure by the upper classes, which typified screwball screen material. Sturges next turned to adapting a Paramount literary property for his first "A" picture, and the results were finally in the screwball mainstream. *The Lady Eve* (1941), while it does move away from the luxury life of the big city during its first half, opts for a pratfall-prone, shipboard romance between first-class passengers on a luxury liner. Sturges' ironic twist lies in the surprise that the blossoming affair, between a naïve young heir to a brewery fortune and the ravishing "daughter" of a cultured older man, is a cover for a bold attempt at gold-digging, because the latter two are actually a seasoned team of card sharks. Sturges relies heavily on the screwball staple of the aggressive woman (Barbara Stanwyck) versus the timid man (Henry Fonda), but doubles the comic frenzy by staging an encore of their disastrous courtship when, after her venal purpose has been revealed, she re-enters the hapless fellow's life under a second, and more exotic, false identity and wins his affections anew.

Sturges' subsequent revisiting of his concerns from the early 1930s was also bigger budgeted, likewise attracted more critical and public approval, and thereby certified his 1941 breakthrough to major director status. *Sullivan's Travels* employed the comic-romantic, cross-country journey of *It Happened One Night* in contrast with the bleak and threatening, socio-political milieu of such "hobo life" classics as *Beggars of Life* (1928), *I Am a Fugitive from a Chain Gang* (1932), and *Wild Boys of the Road* (1933). In the Sturges film, a high-living, guilt-ridden, and overly successful director of movie comedies escapes his golden cloister to sample society's raw and festering underside of homeless poverty. The fictional director's search for "truth," which he hopes to bring to the screen instead of the screwball merriment for which he has become famous, has been taken to be a reflexive statement of Sturges' own artistic concerns, following his achieving professional success. That he weaves his topical satire of "serious" movie making into a defense of the screwball vision is fully consistent with the conclusion that he, and ultimately his screen alter ego, both reach—that raucous comedy is liberating of itself, especially for the unfortunate multitude who view it, and it is in no way morally inferior to serious, social message-infused drama. The cycle of screwball comedy had already peaked by the time it was defended in *Sullivan's Travels*, with *The Lady Eve* in retrospect representing one of the genre's late masterpieces. And despite *Eve's* critical and commercial success, Sturges found he had attracted no imitators, with the possible, half-hearted example of a conventional romantic comedy called *Rings on Her Fingers* (1942), obviously modeled on Sturges' triumph but devoid of its humor.

Auteurist interpreters of the Sturges phenomenon eagerly point to a major dialectic in his personal history to explain his bent for parodying society's aspirations to cultural importance.[27] Raised in the finest continental private schools at the insistence of a domineering mother who lusted after high art, Sturges had instead adopted his stepfather's tastes and become a devoted fan of the common, popular arts—in particular, the pratfall and custard pie world of the silent comedy. Years later, when the younger Sturges' success as a writer led him to the director's chair, he sought not only to indulge this penchant (for all his films are punctuated with slapstick) but also to deflate a wide variety of institutional pretentions and thereby justify his calling to comedy.

Sturges returned to making, rather than defending, screwball comedy for his second 1941 release, and it was as wackily brilliant as anything from the cycle at its zenith. *The Palm Beach Story*'s exercise in separation and reunion (an inventor's wife leaves him, cavorts with the idle rich, and all ends incredibly happily) deserts Manhattan early on for a wild train ride to the southeastern playground of the moneyed and much married, leisure class. Sturges' love of sudden, direction reversing plot twists, given vent in the extreme by the picture's last reel introduction of identical twins for the central characters, then manifested itself in life, in regard to his new Hollywood career.

He intended his next directorial project to focus once more on an inventor. (He himself was one, avocationally, and of odd "gadgets.") But a great and dangerous experiment occurred when Sturges chose to make a film version of *Triumph Over Pain*, a serious biography of a medical researcher whose unselfish (and therefore unprofessional) sharing of his anesthesia formula brought him utter ruin. The book's factual story fascinated Sturges, but he was determined to film its tragedy as comedy, thus remaining true to the satirical screwball vision of life with which he had become popularly identified. Disastrous previews convinced studio brass that the finished film was unreleasable. Sturges' treasured independence at Paramount was curtailed and he finished out his contract by devising a pair of wartime comedies—intended not for any of the sophisticated or appealing stars with whom he had once excelled, but for another studio contractee, the gawky, stuttering, terminally post-adolescent bumbler and misfit comic performer, Eddie Bracken.

Sturges employed his prodigious talent for conjuring verbal and physical frenzy to the extreme in crafting the two Bracken vehicles, both of which wholly eschewed the love-at-first-spite, battle-of-the-sexes, class-conflict-ameliorating approaches of the screwball cycle. Instead, fired by the indignity of losing his Paramount autonomy, he created a pair of genuinely subversive satires of the publicly sacrosanct virtues the rest of Hollywood was upholding valiantly while "doing its part" for the war effort. *The Miracle of Morgan's Creek* (1943) took as a point of departure the excessive "kindness to strangers" of homefront girls befriending soldiers about to depart for combat. Then, it played the resulting pregnancy of one enthusiastic lass into a potentially blasphemous, Christmas Eve "miracle," when sextuplets arrive and a hapless 4-F mistakenly becomes a media "hero" for supposedly doing his "duty." The blinding skill with which Sturges camouflaged this dangerous material via non-stop laughs eased the picture past the censors. It became a considerable hit, though this was not quite the case with his other Bracken assignment, *Hail the Conquering Hero* (1944), which also used the mistaken identity ploy, this time to allow a pitiable, draft exempt nebbish to be acclaimed as a combat hero and elected mayor of the town which bombastically welcomes him home.

Adjusting his choice of story material to both studio pressures and the radically changed national mood, Sturges had felt obliged to leave the urban, upper-class, pretty people of screwball comedy behind him, concentrating instead on the homely eccentricities of small-town, homefront America at war. With his contract completed, Sturges was already gone from Paramount by the time the surprising returns were coming in from these final, hilarious celebrations of chaos. The re-cutting salvage job done by others on his medical research story, finally released as *The Great Moment* (1944), only confirmed the prophecy of its previews, and left open the question of whether heroic tragedy could ever be done justice with a screwball treatment.

Sturges then sought independence in what became a bizarre and stormy partnership with another inventor of sorts, Howard Hughes. Their ill-fated production company, California Pictures, did succeed in coaxing the enormously popular silent comic Harold Lloyd out of retirement for a comeback attempt under Sturges' direction, but the co-producers quarrelled and Hughes suppressed the film. It contained a most overt mixture of multi-layered, verbal fireworks and Sturges' beloved silent slapstick, but *The Sin of Harold Diddlebock* (1946) is most accurately classified as a star vehicle for a once-beloved, personality comic. Its satire of the Horatio Alger success ethic harked back even before the screwball era and was in reality doubly outdated for the tastes of post–WWII moviegoers.

The film's eventual re-cutting and unsuccessful release as *Mad Wednesday* in 1950 came on the heels of two more Sturges failures made for 20th Century–Fox, *Unfaithfully Yours* (1948) and *The Beautiful Blonde from Bashful Bend* (1949). The former was quite devoid of the joy of vintage screwball comedy, opting instead for bitter wit and mordant slapstick as a possibly cuckolded symphony conductor visualizes (while conducting) ways to murder his wife. A latter-day popularizing of "black comedy" eventually redeemed the film's reputation as being ahead of its time, and led to its highly touted remake in 1982. This has not been the case, however, for the subsequent film, which submerged the previously reliable boxoffice appeal of Betty Grable in a slapstick-filled, western parody centering on a female fugitive who repeatedly shoots a vengeful judge in the posterior.

Like McCarey and La Cava before him, Sturges fueled his career downturn with alcohol, as the brief years of his screwball success receded rapidly into history. Abortive attempts at Broadway, television, and Parisian exile then followed for Sturges, until his last film, a curious and gentle, decidedly non-screwball satire on French manners and values called, alternatively, *The French They Are a Funny Race* or *The Diary of Major Thompson* (1957).[21]

These, then, were the principal directors of screwball comedy. Each, as has been seen, combined an affinity for the visual humor of the silent screen with a skill at swiftly paced verbal comedy, frequently set among the leisure classes. All were fiercely independent and sought to control and maintain the integrity of their original or tandem-written scripts, often by freelancing or serving as their own producers. They repeatedly worked with the same collaborators and favorite performers, and auteurist similarities abound in their individual collections of work. With the exception of Hawks, each specialized in comedy, screwball or not, and continued a commitment to making the public laugh throughout their careers.

The balance of this book offers in chronological form (with alphabetical index) a directory of the screwball comedy cycle, 1934–1942, listing title, year of release, major creative credits, performing cast, plot synopsis, and a historical analysis of each film's place in the evolution of this uniquely enjoyable form of movie comedy. Only films which the authors have identified as *primarily* screwball in style are listed, although several related productions are discussed in the preceding text. It is our hope that both devoted viewers and serious researchers of classic American cinema will find this work a helpful tool, either in tracing the cycle as a whole, or in locating and focusing on individual films.

THE FILMS, 1934–1942

It Happened One Night

1934. Directed by Frank Capra. Produced by Harry Cohn. Screenplay by Robert Riskin, from a story by Samuel Hopkins Adams. Photography by Joseph Walker. Running time: 104 minutes. A Columbia release.

Peter Warne — Clark Gable
Ellie Andrews — Claudette Colbert
Alexander Andrews — Walter Connolly
Oscar Shapely — Roscoe Karns
King Westley — Jameson Thomas
Bus Drivers — Ward Bond
              Eddy Chandler
Danker — Alan Hale
Zeke — Arthur Hoyt
Zeke's Wife — Blanche Frederici
Joe Gordon — Charles C. Wilson
Lovington — Wallis Clark
Henderson — Harry C. Bradley
Auto Camp Manager — Harry Holman
Manager's Wife — Maidel Turner
Station Attendant — Irving Bacon
Reporters — Charles D. Brown
              Hal Price

A wayward heiress and a dogged newspaperman meet while she is on the run from her father. They initially dislike each other but gradually fall in love. He plans to exploit their friendship for an exclusive, inside story about her romance with a notorious playboy/fortune

45

Clark Gable and Claudette Colbert in *It Happened One Night,* copyright 1934 by Columbia Pictures Corporation.

hunter. Instead, she deserts her unworthy groom at the altar and runs off with the reporter.

The screwball genre appears to have grown out of the unprecedented success (all five top Oscars) of this comedy clash of the classes. The heiress is impractical, impetuous, spoiled, and reeking of social position. Her reporter-protector-exploiter-redeemer embodies the seemingly opposite traits of practicality, planning, industriousness, and the egalitarian aura of the common man. Their playful, even slapstick interchanges build on both a mutually growing sexual attraction and on the transcendent, Depression-linked, mythic proposition that class conflict is solvable when hositilities, pretensions, and suspicions are dissolved with humor. Capra and company had discovered a powerful palliative with which the movies would seduce millions in the decade ahead. The screwball comedy was born.

Twentieth Century

1934. Directed by Howard Hawks. Produced by Howard Hawks. Screenplay by Ben Hecht and Charles MacArthur. From their stage play based on the play "Napoleon of Broadway" by Charles Bruce Milholland. Photography by Joseph August. Running time: 90 minutes. A Columbia release.

>
> Oscar Jaffe — John Barrymore
> Lily Garland — Carole Lombard
> Oliver Webb — Walter Connolly
> Owen O'Malley — Roscoe Karns
> Max Jacobs — Charles Levison/Lane
> Matthew J. Clark — Etienne Girardot
> Sadie — Dale Fuller
> George Smith — Ralph Forbes
> Anita — Billie Seward
> Lockwood — Clifford Thompson
> Conductor — James P. Burtis
> Myrtle Shultz — Gigi Parrish
> Mr. McConigle — Edgar Kennedy
> Sheriff — Edward Gargan
> Porter — Snowflake
> First Beard — Herman Bing
> Second Beard — Lee Kohlmer
> Flannigan — Pat Flaherty

John Barrymore and Carole Lombard in *Twentieth Century*, **copyright 1934 by Columbia Pictures Corporation.**

The upper-world of the Broadway theatre provides a backdrop for this second key film in the establishment of screwball style, but matters of class are submerged beneath the energetic elaborations of the near hysterical style of performance that would soon become identified with the incipient genre. The Svengali-Trilby relationship between a highly successful stage star and her brilliant but overbearing director-lover begins to unravel as the plot unfolds. She futilely flees his demented dominance of her by undertaking a train trip, with the hope of a new and independent career. He pursues her en route, and the comic madness of his on-board schemes to thwart her plans and win her back spark a screen riot of witty hostilities, peppered with eccentric secondary characters who also become involved in the verbal/physical sparring between director and star.

The unusually rapid pace of the dialogue, delivered by hilariously devious and desperate characters, became, with this production, a major contribution of director Howard Hawks to what would later be known as screwball comedy. As in *It Happened One Night*, antagonism both masks and fuels the fire of undeniable, mutual attraction. Carole Lombard's stellar proof herein that she could play wild, verbal comedy was to free her from the more staid, even soggy material on which she had risen to initial stardom. Within a few years she would rightly claim the title of definitive screwball heroine; her lifelong identification with the genre had begun aboard this Chicago bound train.

The Thin Man

1934. Directed by W.S. Van Dyke II. Produced by Hunt Stromberg. Screenplay by Albert Hackett and Frances Goodrich. From a novel by Dashiell Hammett. Photography by James Wong Howe. Running time: 90 minutes. An MGM release.

Nick Charles—William Powell
Nora Charles—Myrna Loy
Dorothy—Maureen O'Sullivan
Lt. John Guild—Nat Pendleton
Mimi Wynant—Minna Gombell
McCauley—Porter Hall
Tommy—Henry Wadsworth
Gilbert Wynant—William Henry
Nunheim—Harold Huber
Chris Jorgenson—Cesar Romero
Julia Wolf—Natalie Moorhead
Joe Morelli—Edward Brophy
Quinn—Clay Clement
Reporter—Thomas Jackson
Stutsy Burke—Walter Long
Foster—Bert Roach
Police Captain—Ben Taggart

A hard-drinking, fun-loving private detective, who works only as a hobby since his marriage to an heiress, solves a baffling murder case while engaging in clever banter with suspects and police. More interesting than the process of detection, however, is the winningly depicted romantic relationship between the acerbically dapper sleuth and his clever, stylish, and utterly devoted wife.

William Powell and Myrna Loy in *The Thin Man*, copyright 1934 by Loew's Incorporated.

Another foundation stone of the house of screwball was set firmly in place with the unexpected success of this modestly produced comedy-whodunit. Throughout the solving of the mystery we see the engaging spectacle of the well-to-do treating life as a series of amusing games and pranks. The central couple playfully spar with each other both verbally and physically, but it is joyously clear that their love is best expressed as a high-intensity kind of joking, putdown filled fun. The fact that their enjoyment of childish pleasures is based on an enviable level of economic security, while openly acknowledged in the dialogue, disappears behind the foregrounded frivolity. Although *The Thin Man* provided fertile soil (alcohol soaked fun-and-games with the rich; wisecracks as words of endearment) for the seeds of screwball comedy to take root and grow, the film's five sequels followed a different genre path, that of the movie detective film, and are not dealt with in this study.

The Gilded Lily

1935. Directed by Wesley Ruggles. Produced by Albert Lewin. Screenplay by Claude Binyon. From story by Melville Baker and Jack Kirkland. Photography by Victor Milner. Running time: 85 minutes. A Paramount release.

Lillian David — Claudette Colbert
Peter Dawes — Fred MacMurray
Charles Gray — Ray Milland
Charles Granville — Ray Milland
Lloyd Granville — C. Aubrey Smith
Nate — Luis Alberni
Eddie — Edward Craven
Hankerson — Donald Meek
Oscar — Charles Irwin
Otto Bushe — Ferdinand Munier
Daisy — Grace Bradley
City Editor — Charles Wilson
Waiter — Jerry Mandy
Taxi Driver — Warren Hymer
Tramp — Tom Dugan
Hugo — Forrester Harvey
Hugo's Wife — Mary Gordon
Vocal Teacher — Leonid Kinsky

A love starved New York stenographer is built into an "instant celebrity" by a helpful reporter. In a series of articles revealing her recently terminated romance with an English duke, the reporter christens her the "No" girl, for allegedly turning down the Briton's marriage proposal. While the publicity campaign is actually a ploy to rekindle the nobleman's interest (since *he* dropped *her*) the proceedings soon get out of hand. The girl is exploited by promoters, sought once again by the errant duke, and finds she really prefers anonymity and a new romance with the working-class newsman.

Binyon and Ruggles joined the rush to rework key elements of *It Happened One Night* and clearly succeeded with this tale of another reporter who falls in love with his subject, again played by Claudette Colbert. The young lady this time is not a spoiled heiress, but only a working girl. The published chronicles of her private life do turn her into a public figure, however, and much humor is generated by her embarrassment at being "sold" to the curious crowd as some kind of attractive freak. Her new role as a would-be singer at a posh cabaret, despite her meager talents, moves the film into satire, as it shows how sudden fame is often milked for the quick buck. More relevant to the building screwball ethic is her disillusionment in discovering that her now re-attentive duke, who had once wooed her incognito, is really a dull fellow of whom she had been quite well rid. Like her predecessor in Colbert's earlier role, she gladly rejects the world of the privileged in favor of the very reporter who had made her name a household word.

Ruggles of Red Gap

1935. Directed by Leo McCarey. Produced by Arthur Hornblow, Jr. Screenplay by Walter Deleon and Harlan Thompson. From novel by Harry Leon Wilson and adapted by Humphrey Pearson. Photography by Alfred Gilks. Running time: 90 minutes. A Paramount release.

Marmaduke Ruggles — Charles Laughton
Effie Floud — Mary Boland
Egbert Floud — Charles Ruggles
Mrs. Judson — ZaSu Pitts
Earl of Burnstead — Roland Young
Nell Kenna — Leila Hyams
Ma Pettingill — Maude Eburne
Charles Belknap Jackson — Lucien Littlefield
Jeff Tuttle — James Burk
Sam — Dell Henderson
Mrs. Belknap-Jackson — Leota Lorraine
Jake Henshaw — Clarence Wilson
Judy Ballard — Brenda Fowler
Mrs. Wallaby — August Anderson
Mrs. Myron Carey — Sarah Edwards
Clothing Salesman — Rafael Storm
Hank — George Burton
Cowboys — Vic Potel
               Harry Bernard
Buck — Frank Rice
Eddie — William J. Welsh
Lisette — Alice Ardell
Barber — Rolfe Seden

A proper British manservant, far from his homeland, is "lost" in a poker game to a gauche Western American couple who represent the tasteless excesses of the American new rich. Comic situations abound as he tries to "civilize" his new employers while their crude charm affects him as well.

Despite its period costumes and historical setting in the Old West of the American frontier, this beloved comedy classic regularly appears on lists of screwball movies because its themes and style transcend the historical distance. Class conflict, ameliorated by humor, this time pits the cultivated self-possession of a finely mannered butler against the gross self-confidence of his moneyed new employers. Many laughs are generated from both his earnest attempts to teach them refinement and from the effects of their rudely relaxed lifestyle upon him. As in so many Leo McCarey films, alcohol (Charles Laughton has a marvelous drunk scene) is presented as liberating and socially levelling—perhaps an ongoing self-justificatory device from a director known for his own affinity for booze. McCarey's equally famous penchant for on-screen ad-libbing, later to become an important addition of his to the screwball style, also seems to be functioning in some scenes. While Charlie Ruggles and Mary Boland appeared as a team in several other outings for Paramount, those happy occasions were much more conventionally domestic in their humor, lacking the screwball bite of *Ruggles of Red Gap*.

The Whole Town's Talking

1935. Directed by John Ford. Produced by Lester Cowan. Screenplay by Jo Swerling. Dialogue by Robert Riskin. From novel by W.R. Burnett. Photography by Joseph August. Running time: 95 minutes. A Columbia release.

Arthur F. Jones—Edward G. Robinson
Killer Manion—Edward G. Robinson
Miss "Bill" Clark—Jean Arthur
Mr. Healy—Wallace Ford
Mr. Spencer—Arthur Byron
Det. Sgt. Michael Boyle—Arthur Hohl
Mr. Hoyt—Donald Meek

J.G. Carpenter—Paul Harvey
"Slugs" Martin—Edward Brophy
Warden—J. Farrell McDonald
Mr. Seaver—Etienne Girardot
Howe—James Donlan
Henchman—John Wray
Aunt Agatha—Effie Ellsler
Police Lieutenant—Robert Emmett O'Connor

A timid little clerk is mistakenly arrested when a look-alike gangster escapes from jail. The attendant publicity arising from a later, correct identification comes back to haunt the meek paper pusher when the vicious criminal attempts to kill his innocent double and assume the man's identity, but the crook is thwarted by the clerk's new-found courage.

Director John Ford gives free rein to his penchant for broad comedy in this minor loan-out vehicle for Warners' Edward G. Robinson at Columbia, and the results are sufficiently chaotic and irreverent to cross over into screwball territory. Robert Riskin's socially incisive dialogue and the resolute and glowing presence of Jean Arthur as the anti-hero's romantic interest and agent of character transformation presage the populist comedy successes Frank Capra would soon be turning out for the same studio in collaboration with his fellow contractees. This was not Robinson's first self-parody of the gangster character he had defined in *Little Caesar* (also based on a W.R. Burnett story) but it remains the most contextually defined, due to the screenplay's tying it to public perceptions generated by overblown media coverage.

She Married Her Boss

1935. Directed by Gregory La Cava. Produced by Everett Riskin. Screenplay by Sidney Buchman. From story by Thyra Samter Winslow. Photography by Leon Shamroy. Running time: 90 minutes. A Columbia release.

Julia Scott—Claudette Colbert
Richard Barclay—Melvyn Douglas
Leonard Rogers—Michael Bartlett

Franklyn — Raymond Walburn
Martha Pryor — Jean Dixon
Gertrude Barclay — Katherine Alexander
Annabel Barclay — Edith Fellows
Parsons — Clara Kimball Young
Agnes — Grace Hayle
Department Store Manager — Charles Arnt
Chauffeurs — Schuyler Shaw
            Buddy Roosevelt
Andrews — Selmer Jackson
Hoyt — John Hyams
Detective — Robert E. Homans
Operator — Lillian Rich
Watchman — Arthur S. Byron
Man — Dave O'Brien
Saleswoman — Ruth Cherrington
Department Head — Lillian Moore

A stodgy, widowed business executive clearly needs some loosening up from his overly rigid lifestyle, plus a new wife to make his family complete again. His faithful, eventually loving secretary devotes herself to these tasks, though unbidden, and finally succeeds not only in freeing the man from his inhibitions, but in marrying him as well.

Another step on the road to establishing Claudette Colbert as a major figure in the nascent screwball cycle, *She Married Her Boss* was also a splendid first contribution to the genre by another master of ad-lib comedy, Gregory La Cava, whose serious application of Freudian principles to the business of laugh-making frequently resulted in plot turns of major character change via the shedding of self-imposed restrictions. Another soon-to-be stalwart of the screwball world, Melvyn Douglas, essays with aplomb the role of the staid executive who blossoms under the "right woman's" guidance.

Hands Across the Table

1935. Directed by Mitchell Leisen. Produced by E. Lloyd Sheldon. Screenplay by Norman Krasna, Vincent Lawrence and Herbert Fields. From story by Vina Delmar. Photography by Ted Tetzlaff. Running time: 80 minutes. A Paramount release.

Carole Lombard and Fred MacMurray in *Hands Across the Table*,
copyright 1935 by Paramount Pictures Corporation.

Regi Allen—Carole Lombard
Theodore Drew III—Fred MacMurray
Allen Macklyn—Ralph Bellamy
Vivian Snowden—Astrid Allwyn
Laura—Ruth Donnelly
Nona—Marie Prevost
Peter—Joseph Tozer
Natty—William Demarest

Pinky Kelly—Edward Gargan
Miles—Ferdinand Munier
Valentine—Harold Minjir
French Maid—Marcelle Corday

A husband-hunting New York manicurist, desperate to marry for money, shares accommodations and plans with a broke ex-playboy who is also fortune hunting for a financially comfortable mate. Their mutual quest ripens into love, and they gladly abandon potential wealthy mates in favor of each other.

Ernst Lubitsch, in his new post as production chief at Paramount, had this screwball romance specially tailored for the actress who was soon to become the personification of the style, Carole Lombard. The desperation of her character's motivation is carefully captured by Lombard's edgy zaniness, playing off the more relaxed avariciousness of newcomer Fred MacMurray, in a role written for, but refused by, the Paramount contractee who had assayed the unsympathetic second male lead in *The Gilded Lily*, Ray Milland. The surprise appeal of MacMurray as Lombard's co-conspirator in gold digging gives their story credible motivation as they validate the screwball disdain for wealth-without-fun and marry each other instead.

The Ex-Mrs. Bradford

1936. Directed by Stephen Roberts. Produced by Edward Kaufman. Screenplay by Anthony Veiller. From story by James Edward Grant. Photography by J. Roy Hunt. Running time: 80 minutes. An RKO release.

Dr. Bradford—William Powell
Paula Bradford—Jean Arthur
Inspector Corrigan—James Gleason
Stokes—Eric Blore
Nick Martel—Robert Armstrong
Miss Prentiss—Lila Lee
Mr. Summers—Grant Mitchell
Mrs. Summers—Erin O'Brien-Moore
Mr. Hutchins—Ralph Morgan
Mike North—Frank M. Thomas

Salisbury—Frankie Darro
Henry Strand—Frank Reicher
Turf Club President—Charles Richman
Murphy—John Sheehan
Lou Pender—Paul Fix

A successful lady mystery writer, whose zany obsession with solving real-life murders has estranged her from her physician ex-husband, convinces him to assist her on one more case, because of the need on the case for medical expertise. The thrills of the chase, combined with the couple's increasingly friendly bantering, eventually reunite them after the mystery is solved.

William Powell's two picture deal at RKO (the other was a non-screwball detective story) involved him in a pair of attempts to re-create the success he had enjoyed at his home studio, MGM, with *The Thin Man*. The playful antagonism signalling romantic attraction which had enlivened that picture is also on display here, but with another distinctive screwball touch—that of the free-spirited female who both frustrates and fascinates her more circumspect love interest. Jean Arthur sparkles in the role, which is free of the proletarian representative baggage attendant to her screwball related, but populist oriented roles in Frank Capra films of the same era. The doctor and his ex, like Nick and Nora Charles in the MGM series, pursue a killer for sport, for diversion from the comfortable, upper-class world they stylishly inhabit, but she is plainly the aggressor and he the reluctant, bemused follower, setting this overtly screwball *Thin Man* imitation apart from the many other comedy-mysteries of the era.

My Man Godfrey

1936. Directed and produced by Gregory La Cava. Screenplay by Morris Ryskind and Eric Hatch. From novel by Eric Hatch. Photography by Ted Tetzlaff. Running time: 93 minutes. A Universal release.

Godfrey Parke—William Powell
Irene Bullock—Carole Lombard
Angelica Bullock—Alice Brady

Cornelia Bullock—Gail Patrick
Molly—Jean Dixon
Alexander Bullock—Eugene Pallette
Tommy Gray—Allan Mowbray
Carlo—Mischa Auer
Faithful George—Robert Light
Mike—Pat Flaherty
M.C.—Franklin Pangborn
Van Rumple—Grady Sutton
Detectives—Edward Gargan
          James Flavin
Doorman—Robert Perry

William Powell and Carole Lombard in *My Man Godfrey*, copyright 1936 by Universal Pictures Corporation.

A scatterbrained rich girl, searching for a genuine Depression victim (a "forgotten man") as the goal of a society scavenger hunt game, brings home an apparent "bum" she has found in a garbage dump. Intrigued, she hires him to be the new family butler and soon falls in love with him, not knowing he had formerly been of the upper class himself. In a series of bitingly class-deprecating vignettes, his presence in the household is seen to be badly needed, for the crass, selfish, and silly family is totally lacking in self-knowledge or the will to change for the better.

Often cited as the definitive screwball comedy, and the first to be christened as one by a reviewer, this screamingly funny jab at the foibles of the idle rich was both popular and critically acclaimed, meriting nomination for six Oscars. La Cava made full use of the comic histrionics of Carole Lombard, whose character set new standards of crazed behavior as a dimwitted-but-appealing society brat. Powell (Lombard's real-life, still-friendly ex-husband) matched her, blow for blow, as the put-upon representative of acerbic sanity in a mansion which has much in common with a lunatic asylum. The film's passing references to the Depression were rare for comedy of any sort in 1936, and the conclusion, with the erstwhile butler using his concealed business acumen to save the family from financial ruin and to provide jobs for tramps by building a night club at the dump, is a curious nod away from screwball escapism, toward the populist realm of Capra's *Mr. Deeds Goes to Town.* Nevertheless, *My Man Godfrey* firmly established Lombard as the queen of screwball and spawned a host of imitative works.

Theodora Goes Wild

1936. Directed by Richard Boleslavski. Produced by Everett Riskin. Screenplay by Sidney Buchman. From story by Mary McCarthy. Photography by Joseph Walker. Running time: 95 minutes. A Columbia release.

Theodora Lynn — Irene Dunne
Michael Grant — Melvyn Douglas
Jed Waterbury — Thomas Mitchell
Arthur Stevenson — Thurston Hall
Adelaide Perry — Rosalind Keith
Rebecca Perry — Spring Byington
Aunt Mary — Elisabeth Risdon
Aunt Elsie — Margaret McWade
Ethel Stevenson — Nana Brant
Jonathan Grant — Henry Kolker
Agnes Grant — Leona Maricle
Uncle John — Robert Greig
Governor Wyatt — Frederick Burton

Irene Dunne and Melvyn Douglas in *Theodora Goes Wild,* copyright 1936 by Columbia Pictures Corporation.

A young woman, raised by two maiden aunts in an ultra-conservative New England town, secretly writes sexy, best-selling novels. Her unsuccessful attempts to feign worldiness while visiting her New York publisher attract the unwelcome attentions of a commercial artist who follows her back to Connecticut and tries to "liberate" her as kind of a whimsical good deed. Instead, she falls in love with him, discovers he has several hang-ups of his own, and pursues him back to New York. Successfully mastering the art of socially outrageous behavior in the style of one of her own wild characters, she scandalizes the artist out of the unhappy marriage he was fearful of ending, returns home in popular triumph with her pseudonym revealed, and marries her reluctant liberator.

Another gifted performer joined the screwball pantheon with the release of this crowd-pleaser, and her success in the field was quite unexpected. Irene Dunne, dignified sufferer in early-1930s "sacrifice" melodramas and lilting soprano of musical comedy, impressed critics and moviegoers alike with her first-class character change act, under the tutelage of Stanislavsky method veteran Richard Boleslavsky, formerly of the esteemed Moscow Art Theater. Dunne's newfound ability to push herself "over the edge" would be called upon frequently in subsequent outings, but here it was greeted with ecstatic surprise as a genuine first. She was aptly partnered by one of the stalwarts of the cycle, the wry and sophisticated Melvyn Douglas, and the consistently amusing dialogue they share in Mary McCarthy's insider's tale of the publishing world became one more gift to the genre from Columbia contract writer Sidney Buchman.

Libeled Lady

1936. Directed by Jack Conway. Produced by Lawrence Weingarten. Screenplay by Maurine Watkins, Howard Emmett Rogers and George Oppenheimer. From story by Wallace Sullivan. Photography by Norbert Brodine. Running time 98 minutes. An MGM release.

Bill Chandler — William Powell
Connie Allenbury — Myrna Loy
Gladys Benton — Jean Harlow
Warren Haggerty — Spencer Tracy
James B. Allenbury — Walter Connolly
Hollis Bane — Charles Grapewin
Mrs. Burns-Norvell — Cora Witherspoon
Evans — E.E. Clive
Graham — Charles Trowbridge
Magistrate — Spencer Charters
Connie's Maid — Greta Meyer
Barker — Richard Tucker
Maid — Hattie McDaniel
Cable Editor — Howard Hickman
Justice of Peace — Harry C. Bradley
J.P.'s Wife — Bodil Rosing

When an angry heiress' family sues a newspaper for libeling their daughter as the "other woman" in a notorious romantic triangle, the crack reporter in question hires a lady-killer to maneuver the

William Powell, Myrna Loy and Walter Connolly in *Libeled Lady*, copyright 1936 by Loew's Incorporated.

woman into a compromising position just in time for the photographers. The pair find real love instead, much to the amusing consternation of the reporter, whose own much-delayed wedding had again been put off when the scheme began.

An MGM nominee for Best Picture of the year, *Libeled Lady* demonstrated the growing stature of the screwball vision, as the 1930s' leading studio finally joined the cycle in high style, committing as many as four of its top stars to the project. *It Happened One Night*'s Walter Connolly was also called in for another variation on his increasingly characteristic wealthy-father role, directly linking the goings on to their screwball roots. The familiar theme of the bedevilment of the rich by shirt-sleeve journalists serves to turn the plot wheels, but this time it is sexual deceit (William Powell as the hired seducer) rather than sexual antagonism that turns to love, capitalizing on the successful pairing of Powell with Myrna Loy which began in *The Thin Man*. Slapstick was to play a major part in defining the world of screwball, and *Libeled Lady*'s oft-excerpted "fishing lesson" scene ranks with the best physical humor of the decade. The crass aggressiveness of Jean Harlow as the too often deserted bride of down-to-earth reporter Spencer Tracy contrasts effectively with the engaging reserve of heiress Loy, as does the feigned elitist polish of Powell with the working man's elan of Tracy.

I Met Him in Paris

1937. Directed and produced by Wesley Ruggles. Screenplay by Claude Binyon. From story by Helen Meinardi. Photography by Leo Tover. Running time: 86 minutes. A Paramount release.

Kay Denham — Claudette Colbert
George Potter — Melvyn Douglas
Gene Anders — Robert Young
Helen Anders — Mona Barrie
Cutter Driver — George Davis
John Hailey — Alexander Cross
Berk Sutter — Lee Bowman
Swiss Hotel Clerk — Fritz Feld
Romantic Waiter — Rudolph Amant
Hotel Clerk — George Sorel
Bartender — Louis LaBey
Upper Tower Man — Egon Brecher
Lower Tower Man — Hans Joby
Frenchman Flirt — Jacques Venaire
Head Waiter — Eugene Borden
Elevator Operator — Cpt. Fernando Garcia
Conductor — Albert Pollet
French Couple — Francesco Maran
Yola D'Avil
Porter — Alexander Schoenberg
Assistant Bartender — Joe Thoben
Doubletalk Waiter — Gennaro Curci
Steward — Jean De Briac

An American working girl, bored with her cautious and dull fiancé, undertakes a European vacation alone, hoping to find excitement and a new romance. In Paris she soon becomes the object of amorous pursuit by two highly competitive and, unfortunately, rather imperfect gentlemen. Their boyish rivalries for her attention and affection turn into an ongoing contest of ingenuity and ego. Flattered and amused, she continues the game, trying to decide between the married suitor, who assures her his wife will step aside, and his self-inflated rival, whose opinion of himself is enormous. After several rounds of one-upmanship, including some downhill slapstick on the Alpine ski slopes, the latter fellow recants his aspirations to perfection and makes the girl's choice easier.

The amusement of seeing the financially comfortable cavorting like boastful juveniles, abetted with heavy doses of clever dialogue, again worked its magic with Depression-era audiences, in tandem with the Cinderella like aspects of the central identification figure. Claudette Colbert once more played a young woman who successfully aspires to high-class romance, and gets the Parisian vacation for which her previous character in *She Married Her Boss* had yearned. While Robert Young was making his screwball debut as the married rival, dependable Melvyn Douglas, Colbert's former "boss," seized another opportunity to display his characteristic urbanity. The director-writer team of Ruggles and Binyon thus repeated the screwball success they had enjoyed with Colbert in *The Gilded Lily*.

Woman Chases Man

1937. Directed by John G. Blystone. Produced by Samuel Goldwyn. Screenplay by Joseph Anthony, Mannie Seff and David Hertz. From story by Lynn Root and Frank Fenton. Photography by Gregg Toland. Running time: 71 minutes. A Goldwyn/United Artists release.

Virginia Travis — Miriam Hopkins
Kenneth Nolan — Joel McCrea
B.J. Nolan — Charles Winninger
Henri Saffron — Erik Rhodes
Judy Williams — Ella Logan
Nina Tennyson — Leona Maricle
Hunk Williams — Broderick Crawford
Mr. Judd — Charles Halton
Doctor — William Jaffrey
Taxi Driver — George Chandler
Process Servers — Al Bridge
       Monte Vandergrift
       Jack Baxley
       Walter Soderling
First Subway Man — Al K. Hall
Second Subway Man — Dick Cramer

An ultra-determined lady architect, unable to get conventional backing for her construction plans due to sex discrimination, makes one more play for an investor in the person of a practical young millionaire, but only after his impoverished father runs out of credit. The ultra-conservative heir, however, is both suspicious of his father's profligacy and averse to taking financial chances. A scheme to convince him that his dad is comfortably solvent and thus — supposedly to follow the old man's example and to invest in the woman's plans goes crazily awry when the pair fall in love.

Goldwyn's famous, failed attempt to hop on the screwball bandwagon probably suffered from overpreparation as much as from ineptitude. Ben Hecht's original script for a 1935 Miriam Hopkins backstage comedy passed through many subsequent writers' hands before emerging before the cameras in this thoroughly different, battle-of-the-sexes story. *Woman Chases Man*, as telegraphed by the title, employs the increasingly familiar plot premise of a stuffy, inhibited Wall Street type who gets badgered into "loosening up" by a dizzy and/or domineering female. The rub lies in the portrayal of the father as an uninhibited spendthrift and of the son as a tight-fisted, closed-minded, cold fish. The scenery-chewing Hopkins gives the role of the architect her hard driving best, while docile and overly respectable Joel McCrea cautiously takes the part of the target of her initially financial, then romantic aspirations. The pseudo-millionaire father, enacted by the twinkling eyed, rascally Charles Winninger, may be the most harmless would-be tycoon in the entire genre, but his character's desperate attempts to fake success, so that his son will help the lady in distress, probably account for this island of sympathy in a sea of ultra-zany byplay. In one moment of extreme literalness the mad goings-on actually maneuver the main characters out the bedroom windows of the family mansion and up a tree — where at least one shift of the many-fisted, uncredited writing team probably left them while searching for a workable ending to the story.

Easy Living

1937. Directed by Mitchell Leisen. Produced by Arthur Hornblow, Jr. Screenplay by Preston Sturges. Photography by Ted Tetzlaff. Running time: 88 minutes. A Paramount release.

Mary Smith — Jean Arthur
J.B. Ball — Edward Arnold
John Ball, Jr. — Ray Milland
Mr. Louis — Louis Alberni
Mrs. Ball — Mary Nash
Van Buren — Franklin Pangborn
Mr. Gurney — Barlowe Borland
Wallace Whistling — William Demarest
E.F. Hulgar — Andrew Tombes
Lillian — Esther Dale
Office Manager — Harlan Briggs
Mr. Hyde — William B. Davidson
Mrs. Swerf — Nora Cecil
Butler — Robert Greig
Partners — Vernon Dent
Edwin Stanley
Richard Barbee
Jeweler — Arthur Hoyt
Saleswoman — Gertrude Astor

An honest working girl, riding on an open-air bus in Manhattan, gains a free mink coat when it falls on her from a penthouse balcony. A turbaned gentleman aptly pronounces the event to be "kismet," meaning "fate." Her earnest attempt to return the coat to its rightful owner, a Wall Street tycoon's wife, only leads to a wild string of misunderstandings. She is mistaken by various minions to be the rich man's mistress, is furnished with luxurious new living quarters, survives a restaurant riot, starts a stock market panic, and eventually marries the tycoon's handsome son.

While the stream of screwball movies which preceded this frantic send-up of the wealthy probably defused the excitement it might have generated a year earlier, *Easy Living* can now justly be appreciated as one of the finest examples of the genre. Jean Arthur's proletarian princess, partnered by Ray Milland's appealing rich-boy-trying-to-earn-his-own-living, had already become familiar screen presences, as had Edward Arnold in his recurring role as an imperious financial titan. The densely packed wordplay of Preston Sturges' slapstick laced script, the parade of eccentric, language-mangling character actors, and the high gloss of the Paramount production, in the very capable hands of style-conscious Mitchell Leisen, add much to the overall impact of a movie classic which in itself can fully exemplify the contemporary fantasy world of 1930s screwball comedy.

Topper

1937. Directed by Norman Z. McLeod. Produced by Hal
Roach. Screenplay by Jack Jerne, Eric Hatch and Eddie Moran.
From novel by Thorne Smith. Photography by Norbert Brodine.
Special effects by Roy Seawright. Running time: 90 minutes. A
Hal Roach/MGM release.

Marion Kerby — Constance Bennett
George Kerby — Cary Grant
Cosmo Topper — Roland Young
Mrs. Topper — Billie Burke
Wilkins — Allan Mowbray
Casey — Eugene Pallette
Elevator Boy — Arthur Lake
Mrs. Stuyvesant — Hedda Hopper
Miss Johnson — Virginia Sale
Hotel Manager — Theodore Von Eltz
Policeman — J. Farrell McDonald
Secretary — Elaine Shepart
Themselves — Hoagy Carmichael
Three Hits and a Miss

A high-living, hard-drinking, fun-loving, well-to-do, young married couple are killed in a car crash, and their suddenly sober spirits
are divinely informed that their only chance at Heaven is to stay on
Earth long enough to do one good deed. The task turns out to be freeing their inhibited, stuffy, and meek investment banker from his stultifying lifestyle. Their efforts, by supernatural intervention, to teach
him to have "fun" wreak utter havoc on all concerned, but he eventually and happily does learn.

The aspect of screwball comedy which pits free-form living
against the regimented conformity of proper society is intensely
foregrounded in *Topper*. The central couple, gaily portrayed by
screen sophisticates Cary Grant and Constance Bennett, proudly
defy social convention both in life and in death. Their carefree
behavior is directly contrasted by the upright, middle-aged banker
and his prim wife, enacted by the perennially repressed Roland
Young and the effusively intense Billie Burke. When the dead
socialites return for some helpful haunting as ghosts, their invisibility
to everyone but the banker (via extensive trick photography and
flying props) causes a stream of poltergeist-like activity which has the
rest of the cast repeatedly screaming, running, or fainting in terror,

Roland Young, Cary Grant and Constance Bennett in *Topper*, **copyright 1937 by Hal Roach Studios.**

while the privileged movie audience shares the collective joke on the flabbergasted denizens of the bemused banker's upper-class world. Two *Topper* sequels followed in the wake of this film's success, the first (1939's *Topper Takes a Trip*) bringing only the female ghost back into the banker's life for another round of magical embarrassment, the second (1941's *Topper Returns*) introducing the banker to a different lady spirit, who happens to be the victim in a farcical murder mystery.

The Awful Truth

1937. Directed and produced by Leo McCarey. Screenplay by Vina Delmar. From play by Arthur Richman. Adapted by Dwight Taylor. Photography by Joseph Walker. Running time: 90 minutes. A Columbia release.

Lucy Warriner — Irene Dunne
Jerry Warriner — Cary Grant
Daniel Leeson — Ralph Bellamy
Armand Duvalle — Alexander D'Arcy
Aunt Patsy — Cecil Cunningham
Barbara Vance — Marguerite Churchill
Mrs. Leeson — Esther Dale
Dixie Bell Lee — Joyce Compton
Frank Randall — Robert Allen
Mr. Vance — Robert Warwick
Mrs. Vance — Mary Forbes
Lord Fabian — Claude Allister
Lady Fabian — Zita Moulton

A young, upper-class couple suspect each other of infidelity and divorce results. Their mutual attraction persists, however, and each subsequently attempts to foil the remarriage plans of the other. The cheerful cruelties they inflict on each other while engaging in their clever schemes only serve to reunite the pair in what becomes a common cause, and they are reconciled on the eve of their divorce's official starting date.

An easy contender with *My Man Godfrey* for the top spot in the screwball genre, *The Awful Truth* lacks in demented frenzy what it more than makes up for in carefully shaded character insight and warm, romantic feeling. At this point Cary Grant was about to become Hollywood's prime farceur, deposing the long-reigning Robert Montgomery, and Irene Dunne had charmed her way to acclaimed excellence as both an actress and as a comedienne who was extraordinary in the latter category by virtue of her ability to "go wild" on cue. Leo McCarey's careful handling of this remake of a 1920s play and film gave the story the screwball touch by repeatedly assaulting the social proprieties. The husband and wife characters each prove themselves highly adept at scheming to induce embarrassment as they devise ways to ruin the other's half-hearted attempts at a new affair with someone else. These deliberately paced acts of semi-

Irene Dunne and Cary Grant in *The Awful Truth*, copyright 1937 by Columbia Pictures Corporation.

controlled aggression and methodical destruction of another's aspirations are the director's high-class modification of the civilized hostilities which were a hallmark of the Hal Roach comedy studio, where McCarey devised and once guided the classic screen relationships of Laurel and Hardy and company.

Nothing Sacred

1937. Directed by William A. Wellman. Produced by David O. Selznick. Screenplay by Ben Hecht. From story by William Street. Photography by W. Howard Greene. Running time: 75 minutes. A Selznick International/United Artists release.

Hazel Flagg — Carole Lombard
Wally Cook — Fredric March

Dr. Donner—Charles Winninger
Stone—Walter Connolly
Dr. Eggelhoffer—Sig Ruman
M.C.—Frank Fay
Orchestra—Raymond Scott and His Orchestra
Max—Maxie Rosenbloom
Dr. Kerchinwisser—Alex Schoenberg
Dr. Vunch—Monty Wooley
Dr. Marachuffsky—Alex Novinsky
Drug Store Lady—Margaret Hamilton
Ernest Walker—Troy Brown
Mrs. Walker—Hattie McDaniel
Dr. Donner's Nurse—Katherine Shelton
Baggage Man—Olin Howland
Wrestlers—Ben Morgan
    Hans Steinke
Photographer—George Chandler
Miss Rafferty—Claire Du Brey
Schoolteacher—Nora Cecil

A New York reporter's circulation-building publicity scheme regarding a young Vermont woman's "last fling" in Manhattan, before her inevitable death from radium poisoning, goes awry. Her drunken, hometown doctor's misdiagnosis becomes the terrible secret the newsman must protect, when he learns the lady is not going to expire on schedule. After loads of media hoopla are expended in exploitation of "her story," reporter and subject have little choice but to duck out of the country until the publicity storm blows over.

In what could well be screwball comedy's most cynical endeavor, *Nothing Sacred*'s assault on propriety is not directed against the rich and socially privileged, but against the big media they own and control, as well as against that media's self-serving, maudlin aggrandizement of the public's presumed compassion for publicized victims of tragedy. It's all "as phony as a glass eye," the film's epigraph proclaims, and the ensuing narrative goes to great lengths to limn the conniving and deception attendant to competitive journalism. More central to the film's inclusion in the screwball cycle is the delightfully aggressive, even combative nature of the growing attraction between the nominally romantic lead characters. Each exploits the other for distinctly non-amorous ends: She conceals her "wellness" in hopes of a wild time in the big city. He first regards her only as another sob-story device by which to milk the public of millions of nickels and dimes while it figuratively pats itself on the back for "caring." Veteran

Carole Lombard, Walter Connolly, and Fredric March in *Nothing Sacred*, copyright 1937 by David O. Selznick.

screwball player Walter Connolly is the paper's demanding, manic editor, described by the reporter as "a cross between a ferris wheel and a werewolf." The actor portraying the caustic scribe is new to the genre but not to the screen — the driven and precisely spoken Fredric March, whose screwball sparring with his leading lady, as aggression turns to love, bests the calculated embarrassment ploys of *The Awful Truth* with an anesthetizing sock on the jaw. Befitting her by-now established pre-eminence in the genre, Carole Lombard lets her character reciprocate the gesture with glee. The "run-out-powder" ending, on a boat to South America, may be more symptomatic of Ben Hecht's fear of the deep plot-hole he had dug for his characters, than of the cycle itself, which usually reached closure on a much more optimistic note.

True Confession

1937. Directed by Wesley Ruggles. Produced by Albert Lewin.
Screenplay by Claude Binyon. From play by Louis Verneuil and
Georges Berr. Photography by Ted Tetzlaff. Running time: 84
minutes. A Paramount release.

Helen Bartlett — Carole Lombard
Kenneth Bartlett — Fred MacMurray
Charley — John Barrymore
Daisy McClure — Una Merkel
Prosecutor — Porter Hall
Darsey — Edgar Kennedy
Bartender — Lynne Overman
Butler — Fritz Feld
Judge — Richard Carle
Otto Krayler — John T. Murray
Typewriter Man — Tommy Dugan
Tony Krauch — Garry Owen
Suzanne Baggart — Toby Wing
Ella — Hattie McDaniel
Pedestrian — Bernard Suss

When an endearingly mendacious mystery writer innocently
becomes a suspect in a real murder, she deliberately confesses to the
crime, hoping that her public trial will become the ideal vehicle with
which to boost the failing career of her lawyer husband. His earnest
defense of his wife wins her acquittal; she becomes a media celebrity,
publicly perceived as a women's rights champion for supposedly having killed her attacker in self-defense.

Screwball queen Lombard's second 1937 send-up of the era's
journalistic penchant for distortion, exaggeration, and sensationalism
was another Ruggles-Binyon effort echoing the genre's jaundiced
view of front-page fame. Although her leading man was Paramount's
rising, "average guy" star Fred MacMurray as the well-meaning at-
torney, some of Lombard's best scenes in *True Confession* are opposite the veteran John Barrymore, thus doubling the linkage to the
cycle-starting *Twentieth Century*, in which they had co-starred three
years earlier. "The Great Profile's" screen status had declined in the
interim, while hers had risen, and the alcoholic haze which
hampered his later career was integrated into his fictional character
for their screen reunion. Barrymore generates an ample share of
laughs as a loquacious drunk with an all-too-keen interest in the

Carole Lombard and Fred MacMurray in *True Confession*, copyright 1937 by Paramount Pictures Corporation.

murder case due to his own, secret guilt. The narrative's humorous assault on the propriety of the American legal system would of itself ease the film into screwball territory, but it is Lombard's delineation of the daffily fantasy-prone heroine which furnishes the picture's genre identity.

Bringing Up Baby

1938. Directed and produced by Howard Hawks. Screenplay by Dudley Nichols and Hagar Wilde. From story by Hagar Wilde. Photography by Russell Metty. Running time: 102 minutes. An RKO release.

Susan — Katharine Hepburn
David Huxley — Cary Grant
Major Horace Applegate — Charles Ruggles
Slocum — Walter Catlett
Mr. Gogarty — Barry Fitzgerald
Aunt Elizabeth — May Robson
Dr. Lehmann — Fritz Feld
Mr. Peabody — George Irving
Mrs. Lehmann — Tala Birell
Alice Swallow — Virginia Walker
Elmer — John Kelly

The sedate, ordered life of a zoologist is wildly disrupted by a playfully willful and eccentric society girl who finds him amusing and attractive, particularly when publicly embarrassed. Her crazed pursuit of the scholar, with ensuing episodes of gleeful mortification, leads to their joint pursuit, in the woods of Connecticut, of her runaway pet leopard, as well as an important bone, stolen by a rambunctious terrier, from the professor's monumental reconstruction of a dinosaur skeleton. The girl ultimately triumphs in winning her guy, but only after demolishing all aspects of his overly sane, cloistered world, including his impending marriage to his stern assistant as well as his beloved museum exhibit.

While certified through the years as a screwball classic, via retrospective screenings and a substantial body of historical film criticism, *Bringing Up Baby*, with its gallery of peculiar characters and implausible romance between personality extremes, was negatively received when originally released. Katharine Hepburn's ecstatically goofy performance, while a surefire crowd pleaser today, only alienated her further from the 1938 ticket-buying public. The actor playing the victim of her character's disastrous pursuit, Cary Grant, survived the screen setback with less damage done to his boxoffice appeal. Howard Hawks' total inversion of the heroic adventure story

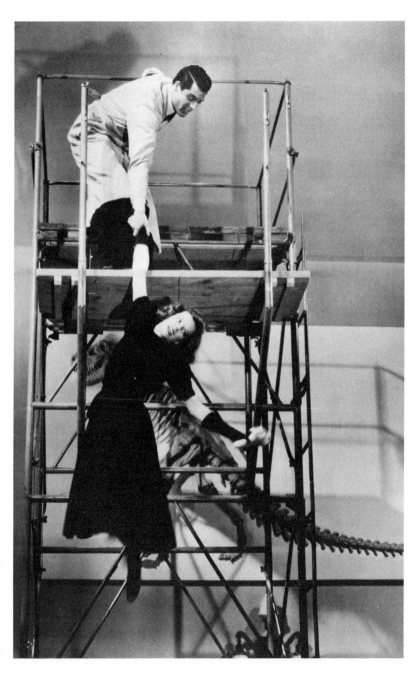

Cary Grant and Katharine Hepburn in *Bringing Up Baby*, **copyright 1938 by RKO Radio Pictures Incorporated.**

at which he also excelled but to more consistent public approval, follows one of the now established screwball forms by having the female's bizarre behavior drive the plot, even to the distraction of all subsidiary characters. The slapstick is plentiful, with destruction of clothing, cars, trucks, other valuable property, plus personal dignity and social decorum in general, taking much of the screen time between innovatively illogical exchanges of dialogue.

Bluebeard's Eighth Wife

1938. Directed and produced by Ernst Lubitsch. Screenplay by Charles Brackett and Billy Wilder. From play by Alfred Savior. Adapted by Charles Andrews. Photography by Leo Tover. Running time: 80 minutes. A Paramount release.

> Nicole de Loiselle — Claudette Colbert
> Michael Brandon — Gary Cooper
> Marquis de Loiselle — Edward Everett Horton
> Albert de Regnier — David Niven
> Aunt Hedwige — Elizabeth Patterson
> M. Pepinard — Herman Bing
> Kid Mulligan — Warren Hymer
> Assistant Hotel Managers — Franklin Pangborn
> Armand Cortes
> Floorwalker — Rolf Sedan
> Prof. Urganzeff — Lawrence Grant
> Potin — Lionel Pape
> Clerk — Tyler Brooke
> Uncle Andre — Tom Ricketts
> Uncle Fernandel — Barlow Borland
> Extras — Charles Halton
> Sacha Guitry

The attractive daughter of a penniless French aristocrat is courted by a much-married millionaire. Her reluctant acceptance of his marriage proposal requires a pre-nuptial agreement guaranteeing her $100,000 per year if they should divorce. Her deviously distracting behavior as a wife subsequently drives her new husband to a psychological breakdown, but pity turns to love, and she is reunited with him after arranging for his escape, while straightjacketed, from a mental institution. Her kiss, at last, gives him the power to break his bonds and claim his wife.

Franco-American Claudette Colbert's apparent practice of working French themes and or locations into her successful string of Paramount comedies continued with this dark and farcical entry, which qualifies as screwball by dint of its assertive and passive leading lady and man, respectively. The major variation on what had become a familiar screwball plot lay in the change from the loony heroine figuratively driving the hero crazy to a scheming woman literally doing the same to her mate/victim. The absolving power of last-minute, true love is employed to redeem the cynical narrative from collapsing under the weight of its own misogyny, following the not very reassuring revelation, which contradicts the film's *Grand Guignol*-style title, that the hero's six previous wives did not die by his hand. Despite scattered scenes of considerable humor, best of which is a department store dispute between the couple over buying only a half-pair of men's pajamas, this is an angrier, colder entry than the rest of Lubitsch's American comedies. Yet it is also his only departure from the comedy of manners into screwball territory. Credit for his excursion ultimately rests with ace cynics Wilder and Brackett—and their fiercely unsentimental adaptation of a French play.

Joy of Living

1938. Directed by Tay Garnett. Produced by Felix Young. Screenplay by Gene Towne, Graham Baker and Allan Scott. From story by Dorothy Fields and Herbert Fields. Photography by Joseph Walker. Running time: 90 minutes. An RKO release.

Maggie—Irene Dunne
Dan—Douglas Fairbanks, Jr.
Minerva—Alice Brady
Dennis—Guy Kibbee
Harrison—Jean Dixon
Potter—Eric Blore
Salina—Lucille Ball
Mike—Warren Hymer
Cafe Owner—Billy Gilbert
Bert Pine—Frank Milan

Dotsy Pine—Dorothy Steiner
Betsy Pine—Estelle Steiner
Marie—Phyllis Kennedy
Orchestra Leader—Franklin Pangborn
Mac—James Burke
Oswego—John Qualen
Magistrate—Spencer Charters

A successful singer, as thoroughly devoted to her profession as her repellent family of n'er-do-wells are to her continuing financial support, is aggressively courted by a free-spirited playboy. Their love-at-first-spite, one-sided relationship leads to his prosecution for pestering her, but his giddy persistence finally wins her over, freeing her from a too ordered life of glamorous servitude to her shiftless family's demands.

The screwball-fantasy lure of defying conventions and obligations keys the action in this tuneful romance which, it if had included just one more Jerome Kern-Dorothy Fields composition, might have been traditionally classified by the film industry as a five-song, therefore genuine, musical. In any case, the witty wordplay of Fields' lyrics are essentially right for a screwball setting, and Irene Dunne elevates her rather conventional role (in contrast to her previous screwball successes) by means of the unveiling of a fine sense of humor as she warms to the child's game ministrations of Doug Fairbanks Jr.'s devil-may-care suitor. Screwball comedy's frequent mixing of slapstick with romance is also operative, highlighted by a frantic game of "crack the whip" at a roller rink. The girl's family, while certainly as peculiar and spoiled as the one in *My Man Godfrey*, generate far fewer laughs as they parade their varieties of pettiness, and are reminiscent of the nasty group of hangers-on who savored their parasitic hold on the Jean Harlow character in the pre-screwball, *Front Page*-influenced, 1933 Hollywood self-satire, *Bombshell.*

Vivacious Lady

1938. Directed by George Stevens. Produced by Pandro S. Berman. Screenplay by P.J. Wolfson and Ernest Pagano. From story by I.A.R. Wylie. Photography by Robert DeGrasse. Running time: 90 minutes. An RKO release.

Francey—Ginger Rogers
Peter—James Stewart
Keith—James Ellison
Mrs. Morgan—Beulah Bondi
Mr. Morgan—Charles Coburn
Helen—Frances Mercer
Jenny—Phyllis Kennedy
Apartment Manager—Franklin Pangborn
Culpepper—Grady Sutton
Waiter Captain—Jack Carson
Joseph—Alec Craig
Porter—Willie Best

A small-town college professor travels to New York on a mission to retrieve his gin soaked brother from the costly attractions of the night club world. Instead, the innocent academic is smitten with a lovely showgirl, who returns the attention so wholeheartedly that they marry on impulse. Trying to fit his new bride into the tightly knit structure of campus society proves a formidable task for the professor, and instead it is *she* who frees *him* from the stultifying grasp of family and faculty.

Like Leo McCarey, George Stevens honed his comic senses on the misadventures of Laurel and Hardy at the Hal Roach studios, but Stevens' graduation to feature films was less free-wheeling in its reaching for laughs. At his best he was, however, quite good at mixing comedy with drama, as evidenced by the semi-screwball tone of some scenes in his famous tear-jerker, *Penny Serenade* (1941). In *Vivacious Lady* the James Stewart character becomes a variation on the customarily repressed, even feckless, screwball comedy male. His need for a liberating force in his life, to free him from his dominating, college-president father and the ivy-covered hothouse he represents, is wondrously fulfilled by Ginger Rogers' loving and life-affirming New Yorker. Yet her fortuitous intervention in the younger man's cautious and controlled existence is more bubbly than zany, more good-natured than anarchic, making her a screwball heroine of a milder stripe. Liberation is still the byword, but it is a gentler breaking down of the tradition-bound walls that imprison the hero than in many other entries in the cycle.

Ginger Rogers and James Stewart in *Vivacious Lady*, copyright 1938 by RKO Radio Pictures Incorporated.

Holiday

1938. Directed by George Cukor. Produced by Everett Riskin. Written by Donald Ogden Stewart and Sidney Buchman. From play by Philip Barry. Photography by Franz Planer. Running time: 95 minutes. A Columbia release.

Linda Seton — Katharine Hepburn
Johnny Case — Cary Grant

Julia Seton — Doris Nolan
Ned Seton — Lew Ayres
Prof. Nick Potter — Edward Everett Horton
Edward Seton — Henry Kolker
Laura Cram — Binnie Barnes
Susan Potter — Jean Dixon
Seton Cram — Henry Daniell
Banker — Charles Trowbridge
Thayer — George Pauncefort
Jennings — Mitchell Harris
Edgar — Neil Fitzgerald
Grandmother — Marion Ballou
Man in Church — Howard Hickman
Woman in Church — Hilda Plowright

A hard-working young man earns a modest fortune on Wall Street, plans to marry upward into a fine family, and to travel the world by combining early retirement with an extended honeymoon. Such a premature escape from the socially obligatory rat race perplexes both the girl and her father, who expect more traditional behavior, but the wedding is still on — until the fiancée's intelligent, but playfully anti-social, older sister catches the fellow's fancy as the sheer personification of the kind of holiday to which he has been aspiring.

George Cukor's stylish and clever remake of a late 1920s, pre-screwball play and film gave to the new genre, with only moderate updating of the story in outlook, a polish and gentility it rarely was to achieve either during the unfolding of its initial cycle or in latter-day attempts at revival. Katharine Hepburn's visible pleasure at tackling the role she once understudied on Broadway invests the older sister character with a supreme confidence in her spontaneous campaign to extricate her sibling's boyfriend from the life-denying, dungeon-home into which he stands in danger of being mentally, if not physically, imprisoned. Until the contrived-but-effective, shipboard conclusion, *Holiday* moves at a rather refined pace, which makes Cary Grant's punctuation of a key conversation with an acrobatic back-flip (an artifact of the performer's mime-troupe youth) such a memorable surprise. The narrative's contrasting of two simultaneous parties, one a fancy-dress affair with the cream of society and the other an intimate gathering in the family mansion's children's playroom, while a carryover from the vintage source material, fits the screwball aesthetic well by virtue of the symbolic rejection of adult sophistication in favor of child's play.

Katharine Hepburn, Cary Grant, and Henry Kolker in *Holiday*, copyright 1938 by Columbia Pictures Corporation.

Four's a Crowd

1938. Directed by Michael Curtiz. Produced by Hal B. Wallis. Written by Casey Robinson and Sig Herzig. Story by Wallace Sullivan. Photography by Ernest Haller. Running time: 90 minutes. A Warner Brothers-First National release.

Robert Kensington Lansford — Errol Flynn
Lorri Dillingwell — Olivia de Havilland
Jean Christy — Rosalind Russell
Patterson Buckley — Patric Knowles
John Dillingwell — Walter Connolly
Silas Jenkins — Hugh Herbert
Bingham — Melville Cooper
Preston — Franklin Pangborn
Barber — Herman Bing
Amy — Margaret Hamilton
Butler — Joseph Crehan
Young — Joe Cunningham
Secretaries — Dennie Moore
Gloria Blondell
Carole Landis

Mrs. Jenkins — Rene Riano
Dr. Ives — Charles Trowbridge
Charlie — Spencer Charters

A dapper public relations executive is hired by a widely hated millionaire in a desperate attempt to improve the rich man's image with the masses. Romantic complications ensue when the P.R. whiz falls for the plutocrat's slightly spoiled, but appealing daughter. All ends happily after the pair escape their previous love interests via a shuffling of the amorous alliances of the four main characters.

At the height of the screwball cycle, no major studio could afford to miss out on the seeming boxoffice bonanza, whether the temperament and or skills of its contractees befitted similar product or not. This picture was a rare Warners' entry in the competition, and the goal of matching the style and sensibility of previous successes made elsewhere was regrettably not met. The inclusion of several familiar character performers from the cycle clearly marked the studio's intentions, most notably in Walter Connally's sympathetic portrayal of the millionaire, whose great pleasure in life is not in smashing the competition, but in racing an elaborate set of model trains. Nevertheless, the picture encounters difficulties in making the rich appealingly amusing in their foibles. Errol Flynn lacks the confidence of his swashbuckling roles, and Olivia de Havilland as the heiress is much more winsome than wacky. The curious choice of profession for the Flynn character, a job only vaguely understood by most moviegoers of the time, does relate directly to the historic campaign a real-life image maker once staged to counter the charge of being a "robber baron," which detractors had leveled against oil-and-finance magnate John D. Rockefeller.

You Can't Take It with You

1938. Directed and produced by Frank Capra. Written by Robert Riskin. From play by George S. Kaufman and Moss Hart. Photography by Joseph Walker. Running time: 127 minutes. A Columbia release.

Alice Sycamore — Jean Arthur
Grandpa Vanderhof — Lionel Barrymore

Tony Kirby—James Stewart
Anthony Kirby, Sr.—Edward Arnold
Penny Sycamore—Spring Byington
Kolenkhov—Mischa Auer
Essie Carmichael—Ann Miller
Ed Carmichael—Dub Taylor
Paul Sycamore—Samuel S. Hinds
Poppins—Donald Meek
Ramsey—H.B. Warner
Mr. DePinna—Halliwell Hobbes
Mrs. Anthony Kirby—Mary Forbes
Donald—Eddie Anderson
Rheba—Lillian Yarbo
Judge—Harry Davenport

The romance of a moderately poor girl and a very rich boy leads to a confrontation between their thoroughly opposite (in both temperament and finances) families. The humanism of her bunch of work-eschewing eccentrics conquers the soulless pomposity of his arms-merchant father and allows him to rediscover the simple pleasures of his long-lost youth—symbolized by a harmonica duet with the girl's grandfather. With even the strongest of social barriers transcended by old-fashioned fun and egalitarian high spirits, the young couple's future together is assured.

Capra and Riskin returned with this picture to the screwball genre they helped found, after tackling grander social and political themes in more ambitious endeavors (*Mr. Deeds Goes to Town, Lost Horizon*). Their re-working of the Kaufman and Hart stage success does preserve the zany humor of the Sycamore clan's naïve attempts at self-expression in defiance of the Depression's exaltation of money as a grail-like granter of deliverance and peace. However, the film's narrative expands the role of the millionaire from that of a one-dimensional villain to a more complex individual who has become trapped and hardened by his wealth. This fits with screwball comedy's frequently sympathetic delineation of the rich as frozen by their assets and in need of thawing out via the warming effect of a return, at least in spirit, to the frivolity of child's play. Jean Arthur is again the working-girl with spunk and cross-class appeal. Edward Arnold, the chuckling king of menacing bombast who portrayed her character's monetary-mogul, future father-in-law in *Easy Living*, essays a similar part here, as the parent of James Stewart's earnest scion of a noble house.

Lionel Barrymore, James Stewart, and Edward Arnold in *You Can't Take It with You,* copyright 1938 by Columbia Pictures Corporation.

The Mad Miss Manton

1938. Directed by Leigh Jason. Produced by Pandro S. Berman. Written by Philip G. Epstein. From story by Wilson Collison. Photography by Nicholas Musuraca. Running time: 80 minutes. An RKO release.

Melsa Manton — Barbara Stanwyck
Peter Ames — Henry Fonda
Lt. Mike Brent — Sam Levene
Helen Frayne — Frances Mercer
Eddie Norris — Stanley Ridges
Pat James — Whitney Bourne
Kit Beverly — Vicki Lester
Lee Wilson — Ann Evers
Dora Fenton — Catherine O'Quinn
Myra Frost — Linda Terry
Jane — Eleanor Hansen
Hilda — Hattie McDaniel
Sgt. Sullivan — James Burke

Henry Fonda and Barbara Stanwyck in *The Mad Miss Manton,* **copyright 1938 by RKO Radio Pictures Incorporated.**

Bat Regan — Paul Guilfoyle
Frances Clark — Penny Singleton
Sheila Lane — Leona Maricle
Gloria Hamilton — Kay Sutton
Fred Thomas — Miles Mander
Subway Watchman — John Qualen
D.A.'s Secretary — Grady Sutton

A debutante reports her discovery of a murder victim to the police, the body disappears, and her peevish pestering of the authorities results in an embarrassing newspaper story about the affair. Her subsequent one million-dollar libel suit against the paper introduces her to the handsome city editor, with whom she shares a hate-turns-to-love relationship as she and a bevy of her society girlfriends try to solve the case in their own, dizzy fashion while the curious newsman tags along.

This highly derivative RKO entry in the cycle features two familiar avatars: the screwball rich girl and the fascinated reporter, while mixing in a defamation case (from *Libeled Lady*) and a comedy-mystery plot (from *The Thin Man* series and *The Ex-Mrs. Bradford*) of decidedly secondary importance to the characterizations. As the mystery unfolds, yet another once-gallant sufferer of early-1930s melodrama, leading lady Barbara Stanwyck, makes her transition to screwball heroine, albeit a couple of years later than her noted predecessors, and rising star Henry Fonda does his best to join the ranks of the befuddled male leads who are led on a merry chase by a female character who both exasperates and attracts them. The unique aspects of the often amusing, though sometimes forced and confusing, proceedings center around the multi-mirror-image effect of the group of similarly excitement-hungry socialites who accompany the Stanwyck character on her "detection" crusade, dogged by the sardonic police lieutenant (Broadway veteran Sam Levene) who firmly believes debutantes have no place in solving murders.

Merrily We Live

1938. Directed by Norman Z. McLeod. Produced by Milton H. Bren. Written by Eddie Moran and Jack Jevne. Photography by Norbert Brodine. Running time: 90 minutes. A Hal Roach/MGM release.

Jerry Kilbourne — Constance Bennett
Wade Rawlins — Brian Aherne
Mrs. Kilbourne — Billie Burke
Grosvenor — Alan Mowbray
Marion — Bonita Granville
Kane — Tom Brown
Mr. Kilbourne — Clarence Kolb
Minerva — Ann Dvorak
Cook — Patsy Kelly
Mrs. Harlan — Marjorie Rambeau
Herbert Wheeler — Philip Reed
George — Willie Best
Second Butler — Sidney Bracey
Senator Harlan — Paul Everton
Rose — Marjorie Kane

A professional writer, while doing research in disguise as a hobo, is hired as a chauffeur by a wealthy family of eccentrics. His sense of propriety intrigues the zany daughter of the clan, and romance results.

The Hal Roach organization attempted to follow up *Topper*, their successful screwball debut, with another vehicle tailored for the newly refined comedic talents of Constance Bennett, whose early-1930's career in RKO melodramas had topped the ranks of Hollywood performer salaries. Borrowing heavily from *My Man Godfrey*, *Merrily We Live* again treats viewers to the spectacle of the super-rich indulging their most childish whims and defying social conventions with glee. The incognito, proper servant who sets things right and wins the spoiled daughter may be a chauffeur instead of a butler and an author instead of a financial speculator, but the *Godfrey* influence is pervasive and obviously intentional.

Topper Takes a Trip

1938. Directed by Norman Z. McLeod. Produced by Milton H. Bren. Written by Eddie Moran, Jack Jevne and Corey Ford. From novel by Thorne Smith. Photography by Norbert Brodine and Roy Seawright. Running time: 80 minutes. A Hal Roach/UA release.

Marion Kerby—Constance Bennett
George Kerby—Cary Grant (flashback)
Cosmo Topper—Roland Young
Mrs. Topper—Billie Burke
Wilkins—Allan Mowbray
Mrs. Parkhurst—Verree Teasdale
Louis—Franklin Pangborn
Baron de Rossi—Alexander D'Arcy
Mr. Atlas—Skippy the Dog
Bartender—Paul Hurst
Jailer—Eddy Conrad
Judge—Spencer Charters
Prosecutor—Irving Pichel
Defender—Paul Everton
Gorgan—Duke York
Clerk—Armand Kaliz

Mr. and Mrs. Cosmo Topper, despite the temporary "excitement" instilled in their marriage (in a previous film) by the party-prone intervention of two fun-loving ghosts, are distressingly bored with each other and heading for the divorce court. Ghostly help arrives in time, however, as the ethereal Marion Kerby (husband George is indisposed) sets up a series of prankish surprises for the staid banker and his gigolo distracted wife, leading to their happy reunion.

Hal Roach's third screwball vehicle for Constance Bennett borrowed this time from his own proprietary material, instead of another studio's hit, but the end product was still a bit shy of the success mark set by the original *Topper*, some two years earlier. Again Roach's long-time speciality, the comedy of embarrassment, predominates and sets the tone, with the middle-aged, upper-class banker the chagrined foil/victim of series of public escapades choreographed (via invisibility) by his ghostly tormentor/benefactor. Again Mrs. Topper finds her peculiar husband a renewed source of seemingly naughty-child "fun" and the marriage is saved. The screwball implication that the rich are often trapped in their social constraints and badly need emotional/social liberation finds eager expression in *Topper Takes a Trip*, along with the Depression-era fantasy message that having fun is impeded by having so much.

Midnight

1939. Directed by Mitchell Leisen. Produced by Arthur Hornblow, Jr. Written by Charles Brackett and Billy Wilder. From story by Edwin Justus Mayer and Franz Shultz. Photography by Charles Lang, Jr. Running time: 92 minutes. A Paramount release.

Eve Peabody — Claudette Colbert
Tibor Czerny — Don Ameche
Georges Flammarion — John Barrymore
Jacques Picot — Francis Lederer
Helen Flammarion — Mary Astor
Simone — Elaine Barrie
Stephanie — Hedda Hopper
Marcel — Rex O'Malley
Judge — Monty Wooley
Lebon — Armand Kaliz

A penniless American golddigger is pursued through the Parisian night life by an amorous taxi driver, while she masquerades as a

John Barrymore and Claudette Colbert in *Midnight,* copyright 1939 by Paramount Pictures Corporation.

countess, crashing a lavish party of the rich and famous. Her charade is secretly sponsored by a wealthy gentleman as a scheme to win back his errant wife, but the arrival of the clever cabbie at the festivities sets the stage for further and more extreme prevarications. His fictitious claim to be the imposter's non-existent, noble husband, plus her protestations that he is insane, lead the pair to a French divorce court, where their "reconciliation" becomes the spark to a genuine union.

This late return to the "Paramount Paris" so often seen in synthetically continental, early-1930s comedies of manners, turns the French capital into a screwball playground, as the leisure class frolics in frivolities and flirtations, while imposter-intruders scheme to take center stage at a glamorous *soirée*. Claudette Colbert shines as she portrays yet another girl-on-the-make with Parisian aspirations, but the surprise is Fox loan-out Don Ameche, whose character becomes even more zany than hers as he feigns insanity as a device to hold her in pretend wedlock under a French law protecting the mentally ill from marital abandonment. This is a clear revision of the genre's standard relationship, which pairs a daffy and often aggressive female with a more passive and confused male. Yet the tone of the piece is intensely screwball, as established by the humorous subversion of the wealthy party atmosphere. John Barrymore makes his final contribution to the cycle he helped begin, wildly ad-libbing and or scene-stealing as the devious gentleman who engineers the girl's Cinderella-like excursion into the cream of continental society, and then savors the deliciously anarchic results.

Good Girls Go to Paris

1939. Directed by Alexander Hall. Produced by William Perlberg. Written by Gladys Lehman and Ken Englund. From story by Leonore Coffee and Joyce Cowan. Photography by Henry Freulich. Running time: 75 minutes. A Columbia release.

Ronald Brooke — Melvyn Douglas
Jenny Swanson — Joan Blondell
Olaf Brand — Walter Connolly
Tom Brand — Alan Curtis
Sylvia Brand — Joan Perry
Caroline Brand — Isabel Jeans
Ted Dayton — Stanley Brown
Paul Kingston — Alexander D'Arcy
Dennis — Henry Hunter
Theodore Dayton — Clarence Kolb
Jeffers — Howard Hickman

A Minnesota bred, college-restaurant waitress, inspired in her quest for a better life by a newspaper story of another girl's windfall breach-of-promise settlement against a high-class cad, sets her sights on a visiting British professor currently teaching on campus. The waitress' plans take several sharp turns, landing her in Manhattan high society before she lands her man.

Alexander Hall, soon to become (although a second-class replacement) Columbia's top comedy director, following the departure of Frank Capra, guided this variation on screwball's cross-class premise. Melvyn Douglas, already as much a veteran of the cycle as Cary Grant, turns in another wryly amused performance as the academic, and Joan Blondell, late of her wise working girl comedies at Warners, makes her screwball debut as the aspiring waitress. In keeping with the standards set down at the studio by Capra, Hall kept the performers firing off the Gladys Lehman-Ken Englund dialogue at top speed, as Columbia scored yet another success in the genre to which it would ultimately contribute more entries than any other studio.

Bachelor Mother

1939. Directed by Garson Kanin. Produced by B.G. DeSylva. Written by Norman Krasna. From story by Felix Jackson. Photography by Robert de Grasse. Running time: 82 minutes. An RKO release.

Polly Parrish — Ginger Rogers
David Merlin — David Niven
J.B. Merlin — Charles Coburn
Freddie Miller — Frank Albertson
Butler — E.E. Clive
Investigator — Ernest Truex
Jerome Weiss — Leonard Penn
Hargraves — Paul Stanton
Mrs. Weiss — Ferike Boros
Doctor — Frank M. Thomas
Matron — Edna Holland
Mary — Dennie Moore
Louise King — June Wilkins
Donald Duck — Himself

When a shopgirl finds an abandoned baby, she soon discovers that no one will believe the child is not hers. The millionaire owner of her place of employment mistakenly concludes that she is the unwed mother of his long hoped-for grandson, and the determined mega-merchant tries to get his playboy son to "do the right thing" by the girl. Eventually the young man does—providing her with a wealthy and attentive new "father" for her "child."

A variation on the "kismet/fate" theme of *Easy Living, Bachelor Mother* revived the shopgirl fantasy of marrying the boss (or his son) which a decade earlier infused memorable silent comedy-romances with such stars as Colleen Moore and Clara Bow. Although the story proceeds at a moderate pace, eschewing slapstick in favor of more subdued gags involving wind-up duck toys and diapering the baby, the cross-class romance is played for both dramatic contrast and humorous embarrassment. Veteran stage actor Charles Coburn made a particularly favorable impression as the millionaire in this picture, giving a new twist to the stock figure, here devoid of the bombast and bluster of Walter Connolly, Edward Arnold, or Eugene Pallette. Instead, Coburn's titan of wealth is more impish, a mischevious, overgrown kid with a single, unshakable idea in his graying head (that the child is his grandson) from which no amount of pleading or reasoning can disabuse him, eager as he is to dote over the "discovered" couple and their "secret" tyke. Ginger Rogers' put-upon shopgirl is not without her wry moments of sarcasm, in the face of unreasoning but well-intentioned attention from the would-be grandpa, but it is with the man's dapper son (David Niven), that she engages in a toned-down screwball romance wherein opposition inevitably is transformed into attraction.

Fifth Avenue Girl

1939. Directed and produced by Gregory La Cava. Written by Allan Scott. Photography by Robert de Grasse. Running time: 83 minutes. An RKO release.

Mary Gray—Ginger Rogers
Mr. Borden—Walter Connolly
Mrs. Borden—Verree Teasdale
Tim Borden—Tim Holt
Mike—James Ellison
Higgins—Franklin Pangborn
Katherine Borden—Kathryn Adams
Dr. Kessler—Louis Calhern

Olga—Ferike Boros
Terwilliger—Theodore von Eltz
Maitre d'Hotel—Alexander D'Arcy

An out-of-work young lady shares a Central Park bench with a depressed millionaire, saddened because his selfish family has forgotten his birthday. The girl's refreshing, direct manner cheers the man up so much that he invites her to be his house guest for an extended stay. Although unavoidable misunderstandings raise suspicions that she is his mistress, all ends happily as her catalytic presence in the household helps the residents shake off their emotional blinders and become kinder people. To cap her triumph, she wins the love of the millionaire's son.

The late 1930's trend to turn down the volume in screwball comedy is most plainly exemplified by this, La Cava's direct attempt to revise the premise and characters of his *My Man Godfrey*. As in much of the writer-director's work, dating back to his silent comedies which fixed the screen persona of W.C. Fields as a sympathetic, henpecked father, La Cava hinges the story on personal liberation from confining emotions. In *Godfrey* the family was so self-centered that its excesses verged on madness and frequently crossed the line into comic lunacy, with chaos breaking out in the drawing room. In *Fifth Avenue Girl* the multi-character, family flaw of selfishness is out front, undisguised by broad humor. Nevertheless, Ginger Rogers' character does puncture the stuffy aura with her near-deadpan candor, and the cross-class nature of the comedy becomes situated within the fringes of screwball territory.

His Girl Friday

1940. Directed and produced by Howard Hawks. Written by Charles Lederer. From play by Ben Hecht and Charles MacArthur. Photography by Joseph Walker. Running time: 92 minutes. A Columbia release.

Walter Burns—Cary Grant
Hildy Johnson—Rosalind Russell
Bruce Baldwin—Ralph Bellamy

Sheriff Hartwell — Gene Lockhart
Murphy — Porter Hall
Bensinger — Ernest Truex
Endicott — Cliff Edwards
Mayor — Clarence Kolb
McCue — Roscoe Karns
Wilson — Frank Jenks
Sanders — Regis Toomey
Diamond Louie — Abner Biberman
Duffy — Frank Orth
Earl Williams — John Qualen
Mollie Malloy — Helen Mack
Mrs. Baldwin — Alma Kruger
Silas F. Pinkus — Billy Gilbert
Warden Cooley — Pat West
Dr. Egelhoffer — Edwin Maxwell

The devious and slick-tongued managing editor of a fiercely competitive Chicago newspaper schemes to win back the professional and personal services of his former star reporter, who is also his ex-wife. Her plans to retire to quiet domestic life by marrying a dependably dull insurance salesman are chaotically disrupted when the editor offers her the chance to cap her successful career by breaking a potential story so hot that it could bring down the corrupt city administration. The wild chain of events which follows, including the saving of a legally insane cop-killer from the gallows, brings the reporter back under the thrall of both the high pressure news business and of her engagingly unprincipled ex-spouse.

The screwball premise of verbal antagonism masking desire, and possibly being motivated by it as well, underlies *His Girl Friday*, although it is far from a cross-class romance, sticking instead to the haunts of a crime reporter's beat and to the shady and cynical denizens of that netherworld. Like several other films in the cycle, the narrative allows a central character to choose romantic partners from between two opposites: the representative of ordered, proper, and uneventful living—or the proponent of chaotic excitement and iconoclastic challenge. The rapid pacing of line delivery with which Howard Hawks helped found the genre in *Twentieth Century* is displayed with even more manic intensity, as Cary Grant does a turn from the more emotionally controlled, or even subordinate male roles of his previous screwball appearances and becomes the unpredictable, out-of-control, engine of plot change previously

Cary Grant, Ralph Bellamy, and Rosalind Russell in *His Girl Friday*, copyright 1940 by Columbia Pictures Corporation.

embodied by eccentric females in many films of the cycle. The role reversal extends to Rosalind Russell's part as well, as she essays a significant variation on the inquiring reporter she first played in *Four's a Crowd.* Despite her character's surface status as an independent career woman, in *His Girl Friday* Russell is actually more pawn than puppeteer, wary of her ex-husband's notorious capability for conning the unsuspecting, but ultimately succumbing to his wily machinations. Ralph Bellamy's part is much less revisionist, essentially repeating his earnest-but-eminently rejectable suitor role from *The Awful Truth,* sans the southern drawl. While much of *His Girl Friday*'s frantic pace and cynical satire can also be found in Lewis Milestone's 1931 filming of the famous play, it is the battle-of-the-sexes atmosphere engendered by making the star reporter female which renders the 1940 version as essentially screwball. *His Girl Friday* may have marked the zenith of top-speed societal cynicism in screwball comedy circa 1940, but strong competition from writer-turned-director Preston Sturges lay right around the corner.

Too Many Husbands

1940. Directed and produced by Wesley Ruggles. Written by Claude Binyon. From play by W. Somerset Maugham. Photography by Joseph Walker. Running time: 80 minutes. A Columbia release.

> Vicky Lowndes—Jean Arthur
> Bill Cardew—Fred MacMurray
> Henry Lowndes—Melvyn Douglas
> George—Harry Davenport
> Gertrude Houlihan—Dorothy Peterson
> Peter—Melville Cooper
> McDermott—Edgar Buchanan
> Sullivan—Tom Dugan

A recently remarried woman discovers she is not a widow, but a bigamist, when her first husband returns from a shipwreck in which he was reported drowned. To set the disturbing affair aright, she undertakes a chaste, trial-housekeeping arrangement with both of them while trying to choose which one to keep. The rival husbands vie for her affections through a series of competitive situations, and the story's ending is comically ambiguous.

The Awful Truth flirted with the Production Code so deftly and amazingly that its lessons (in light of its box office success) were sure not to be lost on other perceptive writers and directors, including the team of screwball veterans, Binyon and Ruggles. The previous film's tantalizing aspects of acknowledged sexual attraction between an about to be divorced couple were played to the hilt, as the mechanical-figurine clock's hands marched toward midnight in the hilarious final reel. Reunion before the stroke of twelve was legal; afterwards, until an official remarriage was signed and sealed, the letter of the law stood in the way of revived connubial bliss, yet it was at this crucial time-cusp that the husband crossed the threshold to his eager wife's boudoir and the narrative abruptly ended. *Too Many Husbands* returned to this edge of forbidden territory (sexual frustration *inside* the bonds of marriage) with the filmmakers no doubt emboldened by the temporary loosening of the Production Code which occurred at the turn of the decade, a move justified as economic necessity by the code authorities to boost sagging film receipts in the wake of the loss of the European market from a Nazi embargo. What qualifies the film as a screwball outing, rather than just a daring sex comedy is the reversion to juvenile behavior of the two male leads. The script's "Enoch Arden" premise, from a vintage play by Maugham, rapidly dissolves into boyish rivalries, with the two grown men bickering with each other over their supposed superiority while engaging in such trivial competitions as spelling difficult words, leaping over furniture, or drawing lots to see who wins the girl.

My Favorite Wife

1940. Directed by Garson Kanin. Produced by Leo McCarey. Written by Samuel and Bella Spewack. From story by the Spewacks and Leo McCarey. Photography by Rudolph Mate. Running time: 88 minutes. An RKO release.

Ellen—Irene Dunne
Nick—Cary Grant
Burkett—Randolph Scott
Bianca—Gail Patrick
Ma—Ann Shoemaker
Tim—Scotty Beckett
Chinch—Mary Lou Harrington
Hotel Clerk—Donald MacBride
Johnson—Hugh O'Connell
Judge—Granville Bates
Dr. Kohlmar—Pedro de Cordoba
Dr. Manning—Brandon Tynan
Henri—Leon Belasco
Assistant Clerk—Harold Gerard
Bartender—Murray Alper
Clerk of Court—Earl Hodgins

A supposed widower with two young children has just married again, after finding what he hopes will be an adequate replacement for the wife and mother who was "lost" at sea. Her sudden return, after being marooned on an island with a handsome fellow survivor, causes the husband no end of emotional and physical complications as he delays starting his new marriage until he can sort out the best course of action. A highly comic courtroom scene precedes the plot disentanglements and proper marital rearrangement.

Leo McCarey's attempt to do a *His Girl Friday*-style sex-switch on his own smash hit *The Awful Truth* was interrupted by his injuries in a car crash and subsequent convalescence. Work proceeded nevertheless, with McCarey as original author and producer, leaving the daily direction of shooting to young Garson Kanin. Many of the gags of the previous McCarey film are re-worked to approximate a similar screwball effect, as the intentionally daffy side of the Irene Dunne character is displayed to first disarm, then win back, the amusedly perplexed Cary Grant character. Dunne even repeats her memorable *Awful Truth* impersonation of a too-much southern belle, and Grant again approaches the film's conclusion, clad in his nightshirt, ready and eager for a code-observing return to his first wife's bed.

The Doctor Takes a Wife

1940. Directed by Alexander Hall. Produced by William Perlberg. Written by George Seaton and Ken Englund. From story by Aleen Leslie. Photography by Sid Hickox. Running time: 83 minutes. A Columbia release.

June Cameron — Loretta Young
Dr. Timothy Sterling — Ray Milland
John Pierce — Reginald Gardiner
Marilyn Thomas — Gail Patrick
Dr. Lionel Sterling — Edmund Gwenn
Slapcovitch — Frank Sully
Jean Rovere — George Metaxa
O'Brien — Gordon Jones
Dr. Streeter — Charles Halton
Dr. Nielson — Joseph Eggenton
Dean Lawton — Paul McAllister
Johnson — Chester Clute
Charlie — Hal K. Dawson
Burkhardt — Edward Van Sloan

A college professor of medicine is incorrectly linked in the press to a rising young feminist author. The erroneous publicity regarding their "marriage" proves mutually beneficial, boosting sales of her new book and easing him into an important promotion. For a time they masquerade at being married out of mutual self-interest, only to find themselves bickering about the kind of trivialties a married couple would genuinely deem worthy of verbal combat. In the screwball tradition, antagonism eventually drops its mask and is revealed to be love, prompting them to "make it legal."

By this point Columbia had become the screen's most reliable supplier of screwball, turning out such minor efforts as this one with only a seeming modicum of effort—and two borrowed stars, Paramount's Ray Milland and Fox's Loretta Young, the latter at last making her debut in the genre after a long string of appearances in the milder forms of romantic comedy. The narrative's cynical view of media publicity combined with the lead characters' surprisingly opportunistic enjoyment of their distorted fame, harks back only superficially to the exhilarating nastiness of *Nothing Sacred*. What is missing here is any real sense of comic outrage at the falsity inherent in becoming a media-created celebrity.

Turnabout

1940. Directed and produced by Hal Roach. Written by Mickell Novak, Berne Giler, John McClain and Rian James. From novel by Thorne Smith. Photography by Norbert Brodine. Running time: 80 minutes. A Hal Roach/United Artists release.

Phil Manning—Adolphe Menjou
Sally Willows—Carole Landis
Tim Willows—John Hubbard
Joel Clare—William Gargan
Laura Bannister—Verree Teasdale
Marion Manning—Mary Astor
Henry—Donald Meek
Irene Clare—Joyce Compton
Miss Edwards—Inez Courtney
Mr. Pingboom—Franklin Pangborn
Nora—Marjorie Main
Julian Marlowe—Berton Churchill
Dixie Gale—Margaret Roach
Mose—Ray Turner
Jimmy—Norman Budd
Miss Twill—Polly Ann Young
Lorraine—Eleanor Riley
Masseur—Murray Alper

Ito—Micki Morita
Marie—Yolande Mollot
Mr. Ram—Georges Renavent

A married couple who lack respect for each other's contributions to their union receive, through supernatural intervention, the amazing opportunity to inhabit each other's bodies for a while, experiencing what the daily routine of life is like from across the dividing line of sex and social roles. Monumental moments of both embarrassment and personal revelation alternate as the man and woman try to act their new parts convincingly in the company of others, until all is set right again.

Hal Roach's screwball success with the *Topper* films led him to try adapting another Thorne Smith fantasy for the screen, again hinging the laughs on upper-class reworkings of the public humiliation gags Roach had built his short-subject comedy empire on a decade earlier, when he exploited popular amusement and empathy over the screen misfortunes of Harold Lloyd, Charley Chase, and Laurel & Hardy. The distinctly sexual aspects of the cross-gender impersonations in *Turnabout* mix class-deprecation with discomforting audience recognition of several then unspoken social taboos regarding dress, physical deportment, and even pregnancy.

The Philadelphia Story

1940. Directed by George Cukor. Produced by Joseph L. Mankiewicz. Written by Donald Ogden Stewart. From play by Philip Barry. Photography Joseph Ruttenberg. Running time: 112 minutes. An MGM release.

C.K. Dexter Haven—Cary Grant
Tracy Lord—Katharine Hepburn
Macauley Connor—James Stewart
Elizabeth Imbrie—Ruth Hussey
George Kittredge—John Howard
Uncle Willie—Roland Young
John Halliday—Seth Lord
Margaret Lord—Mary Nash
Dinah Lord—Virginia Weidler

Sidney Kidd—Henry Daniell
Edward—Lionel Pape
Thomas—Rex Evans
John—Russ Clark
Librarian—Hilda Plowright

A cold-hearted heiress, from Philadelphia's exclusive Main Line district, is about to be married (her second outing) to a stuffy fellow from the same social class. In granting an exclusive, pre-nuptial interview to a magazine reporter, she lets down her guarded, proper behavior, drinks too much, and nearly begins an affair with the suddenly smitten young man. Her new fiancé discovers them together and breaks off the engagement; her ex-husband consoles and advises her on becoming a warmer, nicer person, and the social event of the season (her impending marriage) is saved by the substitution of her previous groom for the one she was about to marry.

Were it not for the opening shot of the imperious heroine being straight-armed out of the frame by her infuriated husband, and for the extended drunk scene, which won James Stewart an Oscar as the adoring journalist, this superbly witty, polished, and ultra-sophisticated romantic comedy would hardly merit the genre classification of screwball. The inside story of how Katharine Hepburn cagily salvaged her failed movie career by inducing Philip Barry to write a play specially for (and with) her, and of how she triumphed with it on Broadway, then sold it (with herself) as a package deal to MGM, has become a familiar anecdote of Hollywood lore. Many of the by-1940 overly familiar and widely disliked (by the general public) Hepburn attributes were grafted on to the fictional character of Tracy Lord, but in the eyes of the love-struck and touchingly eloquent reporter they are re-ordered for mass appreciation as only fitting aspects of a goddess too radiant and lovely to be judged by ordinary standards. Her reunion with her first husband sets things in balance again, after the goddess has been humanized sufficiently by the events of the narrative. With the explosive exception of *His Girl Friday*, screwball comedy had calmed considerably by 1940 from its peak of zaniness in 1937–38, and the fact that so genteel a product as *The Philadelphia Story* is even included in a list of screwball films from its year of release is quite indicative of the transformation.

James Stewart, Cary Grant, and Katharine Hepburn in *The Philadelphia Story*, copyright 1940 by Loew's Incorporated.

Mr. and Mrs. Smith

1941. Directed by Alfred Hitchcock. Produced by Harry E. Edington. Written by Norman Krasna. From story by Norman Krasna. Photography by Harry Stradling. Running time: 90 minutes. An RKO release.

Ann Smith — Carole Lombard
David Smith — Robert Montgomery
Jeff Custer — Gene Raymond
Chuck Benson — Jack Carson
Mr. Custer — Philip Merivale
Mrs. Custer — Lucile Watson
Sammy — William Tracy
Mr. Deever — Charles Halton
Mrs. Krauscheimer — Esther Dale
Martha — Emma Dunn
Proprietor of Lucy's — William Edmunds
Gertie — Betty Compson
Gloria — Patricia Farr
Lily — Adele Pearce

A happily married, successful lawyer and his wife have their domestic peace shattered by the discovery that their union, due to a technicality, was never legal. Doubts about whether, in the cold light of their new-found freedom, they would eagerly choose each other again turn their state of bliss to one of suspicion and emotional conflict. They fight, separate, and fitfully try to sample the single life again with new romantic interests, only to find that the couple's attraction to each other is as strong as ever.

Norman Krasna's story and screenplay, obviously written under the influence of *The Awful Truth,* had been sold to RKO and shelved there for some two years, during which time the screwball cycle had peaked and was waning. The personal friendship between Carole Lombard and her one-time neighbor, Alfred Hitchcock, led to their planning to do a film together at RKO, and *Mr. and Mrs. Smith* was the vehicle on which they agreed to work. It marked Lombard's return to screwball form after a career reversion to more serious drama in her recent pictures, and it went on to be known as Hitchcock's only outright comedy of the sound era. Krasna's variation on Leo McCarey's original plot substituted the discovery of a non-legal marriage for an impending final divorce decree, but the quarreling between the spouses, their futile attempts to start new romances, the man's early determination to renew the marriage, and the plot resolution at an isolated location (a ski resort cabin instead of a cabin in the woods) make *Mr. and Mrs. Smith* almost as closely related to *The Awful Truth* as was *My Favorite Wife.* An important difference, however, can be found in the screwball attributes of the leading lady's character. Whereas in the two previous films Irene Dunne assumed an intentional air of zaniness when the plot required her character to disrupt social propriety and thereby re-attract her former mate, the Lombard character in *Mr. and Mrs. Smith* is actually less zany than in her previous screwball incarnations. Physical-humor situations still involve her, such as a rain shower on a stuck ferris wheel, but she is emotionally better balanced than either her hypochondriac husband (Robert Montgomery) or her cowardly new boyfriend (Gene Raymond). The cabin-bound reunion which closes the film is particularly reminiscent of its direct predecessors, with the crossing of skis in a final shot standing in for the attraction of the clock figurines to each other at the ending of *The Awful Truth.*

The Lady Eve

1941. Directed by Preston Sturges. Produced by Paul Jones. Written by Preston Sturges. From story by Monkton Hoffe. Photography by Victor Milner. Running time: 97 minutes. A Paramount release.

Jean/Eve — Barbara Stanwyck
Charles Pike — Henry Fonda
Colonel Harrington — Charles Coburn
Mr. Pike — Eugene Pallette
Muggsy Murgatroyd — William Demarest
Sir Alfred — Eric Blore
Gerald — Melville Cooper
Martha — Martha O'Driscoll
Mrs. Pike — Janet Beecher
Burrows — Robert Greig
Gertrude — Dora Clement
Pike's Chef — Luis Alberni
Bartender — Frank Moran
Party Guests — Evelyn Beresford
           Arthur Stewart Hall
Piano Tuner — Harry Rosenthal
Lawyers — Julius Tannen
           Arthur Hoyt
Stewards — Jimmy Conlin
           Al Bridge
           Vic Potel

A crafty lady cardsharp lures the timid, bookish heir to a brewery fortune into a crooked game of chance while traveling on board a luxury liner. When love blossoms between the pair, it is thwarted by the man's secret discovery of the woman's shady profession. He falsely proclaims he had faked his affection for her, and in her outrage, she schemes to win him back under a false identity, then spurn him in revenge. She succeeds all too well, tries to shock him with lurid fictions about her sexual "past," and finally gives in to the genuine love they have come to share. Since his passionate avocation is the scholarly study of snakes, the couple sail off together on his next far-flung expedition.

The aggressive, even malicious courtship, punctuated by violent slapstick, which characterized several earlier screwball comedies, returned to the screen with a hearty pratfall in this late entry. The antagonistic attraction which the characters played by Fonda and

Charles Coburn and Henry Fonda in *The Lady Eve,* **copyright 1941 by Paramount Pictures Corporation.**

Stanwyck displayed for each other in *The Mad Miss Manton* (1938) is both multiplied and complicated in Preston Sturges' writing and directing of *The Lady Eve.* Fonda's character literally falls all over himself repeatedly as he reacts to the lady's charms, and Stanwyck's character is less the scatterbrain of early screwball and more of a conniving manipulator of men. Instead of performing his familiar role as the blustering parent of an heiress, Eugene Pallette grumbles and fumes as the young *man's* father. Sarcastic commentary on the proceedings is spoken by William Demarest, the character actor best known for his portrayals of hard-to-impress, working-class, Irish-Americans.

Although some writers have seen fit to lump the whole body of Preston Sturges' directorial work into the screwball genre, close examination of his career reveals that the films he directed prior to *The Lady Eve* are better described as topical satires, rich in verbal fencing and peppered with slapstick, but not yet finely attuned to the sexual conflict and benign foolishness of the elite so central to the screwball vision. The fact that his first directing projects were of unproduced screenplays he had written in the early 1930s, before the screwball cycle had become apparent, may help to clarify this distinction. It should also be noted that Sturges reverted to topical satire after only one additional screwball outing (*The Palm Beach Story*, 1942) and his final, alleged entry in the genre (*Unfaithfully Yours*, 1948) was both *film noir*-influenced and produced well after the screwball cycle had ended.

That Uncertain Feeling

1941. Directed and produced by Ernst Lubitsch. Written by Walter Reisch and Donald Ogden Stewart. From play by Victorien Sardou and Emile de Najac. Photography by George Barnes. Running time: 84 minutes. An Ernst Lubitsch/Sol Lesser/United Artists release.

Jill Baker — Merle Oberon
Larry Baker — Melvyn Douglas
Sebastien — Burgess Meredith
Dr. Vengard — Alan Mowbray
Margie Stalling — Olive Blakeney
Jones — Harry Davenport
Sally — Eve Arden
Kafka — Sig Rumann
Butler — Richard Carle
Maid — Mary Currier
Nurse — Jean Fenwick

A stuffy, successful, and insensitive insurance executive neglects his bored, beautiful, young wife to the extent that she begins an affair with a hot tempered but cowardly, acerbic, possibly deranged, and musically obscure concert pianist. The newly attentive husband tries a variety of schemes to derail his wife's plans for divorce, all the while assuming a stance of "mature" acquiescence and even active cooperation.

Ernst Lubitsch's first wholly freelance Hollywood project marked his second (and definitely funnier than *Bluebeard's Eighth Wife*) attempt at screwball. Despite the contemporary New York setting of the Walter Reisch-adapted screenplay by *The Philadelphia Story's*

Donald Ogden Stewart, the source was the director's own silent hit, *Kiss Me Again* (1925), itself based on a Parisian "boulevard" stage farce of the 1800s in which Eleanora Duse had once starred. What may have made the project appear timely for the screwball cycle was the *Awful Truth*-like plot device of a husband's seeking to foil his wife's remarriage plans on the eve of their divorce. Melvyn Douglas is, for the most part, as suave as ever, but the story does allow him a few lapses into more crude behavior, such as his slugging and pulling a gun on his romantic rival during a dispute over the errant wife. The physical-combat episodes in previous screwball films are echoed in the sequence in which the supposedly cooperative husband is asked to provide divorce evidence by hitting his spouse in the presence of witnesses. The "comedy of manners" sensibility which had long permeated the director's work made the hero of *Kiss Me Again* totally unable to strike his wife, but the husband (Melvyn Douglas) in the remake dutifully complies with the request after downing a few stiff drinks. Screwball's challenge to cultural propriety functions in *That Uncertain Feeling* in several ways, among them the mordant peevishness and impulsively childish antics of the serious musician (Burgess Meredith), the cartoonish representation and ridicule of a "modern art" portrait of him, and the fey delivery of Freudian counselling by Alan Mowbray's Manhattan psychoanalyst. The dashing back to the boudoir celebration of the divorce's cancellation, while pre-existing in the film's source material, gains relevance to the screwball cycle by means of its recurrence in previous films on this timeline, even as recent as *Mr. and Mrs. Smith*, released barely two weeks earlier.

Topper Returns

1941. Directed by Roy Del Ruth. Produced by Hal Roach. Written by Jonathan Latimer and Gordon Douglas. From characters from a Thorne Smith novel. Photography by Norbert Brodine. Special effects by Roy Seawright. Running time: 95 minutes. A United Artists release.

Gail Richards — Joan Blondell
Cosmo Topper — Roland Young
Ann Carrington — Carole Landis

Mrs. Topper—Billie Burke
Bob—Dennis O'Keefe
Maid—Patsy Kelly
Mr. Carrington—H.B. Warner
Chauffeur—Eddie Anderson
Dr. Jeris—George Zucco
Sergeant Roberts—Donald MacBride
Lillian—Rafaela Ottiano
Rama—Trevor Bardette

The Cosmo Toppers, ever the representatives of upper-class conservatism and propriety, are plagued by yet another ghostly intervention. Again, the prim yet flighty Mrs. Topper is baffled by the bizarre behavior of her milquetoast mate as the invisible intruder coerces him into embarrassing situations. This time the objective is not simply to have fun, but to solve a young girl's murder in an isolated, mysterious mansion.

Eager to score another box-office hit after branching out into generally less-successful formulae, the Hal Roach Studios resurrected Thorne Smith's *Topper* characters for yet another screwball go-round. This re-working of the material included one particularly major alteration: The playful female spirit who bedevils the proper banker is not the svelte, sophisticated Marion Kerby (Constance Bennett) of the earlier films, but buxom, working-girl Gail Richards (Joan Blondell), as the rightfully upset murder victim, anxious that her killer be brought to justice. On hand to counterpoint Blondell's sarcastic and slightly shopworn charm is Roach contractee Carole Landis, in the more winsome ingenue role of the victim's surviving best friend. While disturbing the staid existence of Mr. Topper is still the main order of business, the influence of the recent popularity of Paramount's *The Ghost Breakers* (1940) and other revivals of the *Old Dark House*-style comedy-mystery formula can also be detected in *Topper Returns*.

The Devil and Miss Jones

1941. Directed by Sam Wood. Produced by Frank Ross. Written by Norman Krasna. Photography by Harry Stradling. Running time: 92 minutes. An RKO release.

Mary Jones — Jean Arthur
John P. Merrick — Charles Coburn
Joe O'Brien — Robert Cummings
Hooper — Edmund Gwenn
Elizabeth Ellis — Spring Byington
George — S.Z. Sakall
Detective — William Demarest
Allison — Walter Kingsford
Harrison — Montagu Love
Oliver — Richard Carle
Needles — Charles Waldron
Withers — Edwin Maxwell
Police Sergeant — Edward McNamara
Tom Higgins — Robert Emmett Keane
Customer — Florence Bates

A wealthy department-store owner assumes the disguise of a novice, older worker, with the following objectives: to view life from the other side, to determine the cause of recent labor unrest, and to locate and deal with the union agitator who has been stirring up the rank and file. A spunky, outspoken girl clerk befriends him, while unaware of his true status, and provides the curious boss with a surprising dose of bargain basement-level class consciousness.

As did his screenplay for *Bachelor Mother* (1939), Norman Krasna's *The Devil and Miss Jones* uses a big-city department store (such as the one in which he once toiled) as its setting. The performer who made the strongest impression in the earlier film, Charles Coburn, plays a return engagement in a similar role — the store's amusingly cantankerous proprietor. Jean Arthur does yet another turn on her familiar working-girl characterization, in a part which has her cast as the foil for the old man's probing questions into the everyday life of his employees. Her boyfriend, it turns out, is the labor organizer (Robert Cummings) about whom the boss has become very concerned. By means of the humor of contrast, drawn from the cross-class clash, complicated by mistaken identity, the screwball atmosphere is established, and the disguised millionaire learns to loosen his stiff sense of propriety by mingling with the proletariat, as did his tycoon predecessor in *You Can't Take It with You* (1938). The Capra influence may be even more extensive, in light of the amelioration the film tries to spread over the societally endemic capital-labor conflict, which was erupting afresh in 1941 America.

The Bride Came C.O.D.

1941. Directed by William Keighley. Produced by Hal B. Wallis. Written by Julius J. Epstein and Philip G. Epstein. From story by Kenneth Earl and M.M. Musselman. Photography by Ernest Haller. Running time: 92 minutes. A Warner Brothers-First National release.

Steve Collins — James Cagney
Joan Winfield — Bette Davis
Tommy Keenan — Stuart Erwin
Allen Brice — Jack Carson
Peewee — George Tobias
Lucius K. Winfield — Eugene Pallette
Pop Tolliver — Harry Davenport
Sheriff McGee — William Frawley
Hinkley — Edward Brophy
Judge Sobler — Harry Holman
Reporters — Chick Chandler
Keith Douglas
Herbert Anderson
Keenan's Pilot — DeWolfe (William) Hopper

Bette Davis and James Cagney in *The Bride Came C.O.D.*, copyright 1941 by Warner Bros.-First National Incorporated.

A runaway heiress, intending to marry an unctuous dance-band leader of whom her father disapproves, is kidnapped by a daring young pilot hired by the old man. Antagonism gives way to amour, but only after the couple endures several comic indignities while stranded in a desert, following a forced landing.

The comparisons to *It Happened One Night* were obvious and unavoidable, despite the seven years (and several other imitations) which had occurred since the original appeared. Eugene Pallette's role as the girl's flustered father added an even greater sense of *déjà vu* to the picture, but nevertheless it was popular with audiences, who were willing to overlook the frequently forced humor and somewhat inappropriate age of the leads (Cagney was 42, Davis 33 and hardly convincing as a debutante). Not only was *The Bride Came C.O.D.* a reversion to the earliest screwball plot, but it was also performed at a rather high decibel level, in contrast to the mellowing of the screwball style in the last years before the approaching war.

Here Comes Mr. Jordan

1941. Directed by Alexander Hall. Produced by Everett Riskin. Written by Sidney Buchman and Seton I. Miller. From play by Harry Segall. Photography by Joseph Walker. Running time: 93 minutes. A Columbia release.

Joe Pendleton—Robert Montgomery
Bette Logan—Evelyn Keyes
Mr. Jordan—Claude Rains
Julia Farnsworth—Rita Hayworth
Messenger 7013—Edward Everett Horton
Max Corkle—James Gleason
Tony Abbott—John Emery
Inspector Williams—Donald MacBride
Lefty—Don Costello
Sisk—Halliwell Hobbes
Bugs—Benny Rubin

A mix-up by a heavenly messenger (the grandly fumbling E.E. Horton) results in a prizefighter's spirit being prematurely removed from his body, which has already been cremated by the time the

Robert Montgomery in *Here Comes Mr. Jordan,* **copyright 1941 by Columbia Pictures Corporation.**

mistake is discovered. To make amends, Heaven's official soul-transport officer (the elegant Claude Rains) allows the boxer's spirit to inhabit first the body of a recently murdered playboy-swindler, then that of a rival boxer shot down by gangsters. Along the way, the leading character finds love with the daughter of one of the swindler's victims and reunites with a very baffled former fight manager.

What qualifies this supernatural comedy as screwball is its repeated disruption of social dignity, restraint, and associated conformity, by the transmogrified soul of the crude but lovable boxer. Incarnated in the body of a smooth, classy crook and surrounded by the trappings of ill-gotten wealth, the fighter's direct and colorful demeanor engender the style and value conflicts for which the genre had become well known. Although James Gleason's confused and distraught fight manager lacks the privileged composure of a Cosmo Topper, Gleason's character displays some of the same kind of laugh-getting exasperation when he is confronted by manifestations "from beyond." *Turnabout* is another noted entry in the spirit-humor mode to which *Here Comes Mr. Jordan* directly relates, by virtue of its comic savoring of the discomforts suffered by a soul attempting to accustom itself to a new body. Conversely, the picture's great success was followed by a later cycle of thematic imitations and re-workings, including *A Guy Named Joe* (1943), *Angel on My Shoulder* (1946), *Down to Earth* (1947) and *Montana Mike/Heaven Only Knows* (1947), without the inspired touch of screwball which gives *Mr. Jordan* its bite. The fact that Robert Montgomery was given the lead as the boxer, surely a casting against type, followed narrowly on the heels of his acting coup in *The Earl of Chicago* (1940) as an American gangster whose speech and behavior stand in stark contrast to the austere, castle-style living he is expected to endure and continue when he inherits a British title plus estate from a distant relative.

Unfinished Business

1941. Directed and produced by Gregory La Cava. Written by Eugene Thackery. Photography by Joseph Valentine. Running time: 94 minutes. A Universal release.

Nancy Andrews — Irene Dunne
Tommy Duncan — Robert Montgomery
Steve Duncan — Preston Foster
Elmer — Eugene Pallette
Frank — Dick Foran
Aunt Mathilda — Esther Dale
Billy Ross — Walter Catlett
Richard — Richard Davies
Katy — Katharyn Adams
Uncle — Samuel S. Hinds
Clarisse — June Clyde
Sheila — Phyllis Barry

An aspiring singer, on a train to New York for an opera audition, has a whirlwind affair with a too-charming producer. After he quickly dumps her, she fails the tryout and settles for second-best on both fronts — a job singing telephone greetings, then marriage to the producer's younger brother. The comedy temporarily gives way to melodrama when her unresolved regrets and his excessive drinking part them, but they are reunited backstage at the opera, where she has become a member of the chorus.

Forever a Freudian, La Cava here tries out his favorite liberation from troubling memories theme on the critically acclaimed, calculated zaniness of Irene Dunne, in a star vehicle crafted to give the lady the ample singing room to which she and her fans had long been accustomed. Perennial screen playboy Robert Montgomery is more dipsomaniacal than usual, but this can likely be read (as with Leo McCarey) to be a reflection of the director's own fixation on alcohol's personality-altering effects. Society drunk scenes, when played for laughs, were frequently on view in the world of screwball, and the sudden, consolation marriage of Dunne's character to Montgomery's, while not a prime example, does follow in this tradition. However, her painful obsession with the memory of his heartless brother somewhat cools the silly charm of the new couple's downing too many "whiz-booms" just prior to taking the plunge. While the somber interlude in the narrative may actually be more dramatically impressive than its screwball context, it is the latter by which the film qualifies here. Even though the picture's reputation has suffered through the years, it was successful enough to prompt a direct follow-up, *Lady in a Jam* (1942), with the same studio, director, writer, and star.

You Belong to Me

1941. Directed and produced by Wesley Ruggles. Written by Claude Binyon. From story by Dalton Trumbo. Photography by Joseph Walker. Running time: 95 minutes. A Columbia release.

Helen Hunt — Barbara Stanwyck
Peter Kirk — Henry Fonda
Billings — Edgar Buchanan
Vandemer — Roger Clark
Emma — Ruth Donnelly
Moody — Melville Cooper
Joseph — Ralph Peters
Ella — Maude Eburne
Minnie — Rene Riano
Eva — Ellen Lowe
Doris — Mary Treen
Robert Andrews — Gordon Jones
Desk Clerk — Fritz Feld

Barrows—Paul Harvey
Smithers—Harold Waldridge
Ski Patrolmen—Lloyd Bridges
Stanley Brown
Kuckel—Jack Norton
Blemish—Larry Parks
Clerk—Grady Sutton
Necktie Woman—Georgia Caine

The marital bliss of a wealthy, man-about-town and his career-woman wife is sorely tried by his suspicions regarding all the other men in her life. The problem arises out of her job—she is a lady physician with many male patients. He tries to stem his jealousy and gain self-respect by taking a job as a department store clerk, but his playboy identity is discovered by resentful workers who accuse him of "stealing" a poor man's job. Happiness is assured for all when he turns philanthropist, donating much of his fortune to build a hospital, with his wife as chief of the medical staff.

Screwball comedy began its run with affectionate lampooning of the romantic squabbles of the idle rich, the stories infused by a comforting mythology that money may bring on fits of laughable lunacy but it could not buy happiness, thus allowing the more troubling aspects of class conflict in such narratives to be ameliorated, if not obliterated by the gags, witticisms, and pratfalls which lead to the romantic clinch at fade-out time. However, the original story of *You Belong to Me* was written by veteran Hollywood "Red" Dalton Trumbo, and it dares to peel back the protective veneer of sophistication for a rare movie-glimpse at working-class rage. The rewrite by Claude Binyon (his final collaboration with Wesley Ruggles) only softens, but does not deny, Trumbo's acknowledgment of the festering social infrastructure beneath the Art-Deco designs and Algonquin Roundtable-style witticisms so highly polished in many films of this sort. Norman Krasna's shopgirl-screwball entries did pave the way, but *You Belong to Me* makes the recondite acrimony palpable as playboy Henry Fonda comes to resent wife Barbara Stanwyck's hard-won success, only to become the object of much more hateful emotions from the common folk when he sets foot on the ground floor of the workplace. The couple's marital clash, however, is played for laughs, and in a Capra-esque finale, the solution comes in the form of a charitable giveaway which benefits all concerned.

The Feminine Touch

1941. Directed by W.S. Van Dyke II. Produced by Joseph L. Mankiewicz. Written by George Oppenheimer, Edmund L. Hartmann and Ogden Nash. Photography by Ray June. Running time: 97 minutes. An MGM release.

Julie Hathaway — Rosalind Russell
John Hathaway — Don Ameche
Nellie Woods — Kay Francis
Elliott Morgan — Van Heflin
Captain Makepeace Liveright — Donald Meek
Rubberlegs Ryan — Gordon Jones
Shelly Mason — Henry Daniell
Freddie Bond — Sidney Blackmer
Dean Hutchinson — Grant Mitchell
Brighton — David Clyde

A stuffy college professor writes a highly theoretical manuscript on the phenomenon of sexual jealousy. When a major popular-book publisher decides to give the ponderous tome a saturation release for a wide audience (after appropriate editorial simplification for the masses) the author and his wife are invited to Manhattan to begin a national promotion campaign. The lady is then pursued by the lusty publisher and suspects her husband of a big-city dalliance as well — all of this putting severe strain on both the professor's theories and his marriage. His instinctive decision to react like a normal, jealous husband sets matters straight.

Overall, MGM was not very successful at the art of screwball, and its purely farcical romances, such as *Love Crazy* (1941) are outside the scope of this study. In filming *The Feminine Touch,* however, solid craftsman "Woody" Van Dyke, aided by a fine cast and a writing crew which included eccentric wordsmith Ogden Nash, did make the grade with a send-up of the high-class publishing world. Screwball's arch-figure of the calcified emotional state, the college professor comes in line for more barbed kidding and loosening up in the person of serious and sincere Don Ameche, borrowed from his usual run of modest musicals and minor spectacles at 20th Century–Fox. Peripatetic Rosalind Russell, already specializing in strong but susceptible female characters, such as her Hildy Johnson in *His Girl Friday,* gives the role of the "Gotham-discovered" spouse just the right mix of pride and amusement to make the wife by far the film's most interesting figure. True to form, the comedy is mainly at the expense of the professor's faulty theorizing about an intense emotional state in which he has only been a brief tourist at best. The propriety and pomposity of the academy, still at the time closely associated with the elitism, if not the prosperity, of the rich, gets the screwball ribbing much of the non college-degreed, public majority felt was probably deserved, even though the millionaire-baiting days of the Depression were already receding into a pre-war past.

Two-Faced Woman

1941. Directed by George Cukor. Produced by Gotfried Reinhardt. Written by S.N. Behrmkan, Salka Viertel and George Oppenheimer. From play by Ludwig Fulda. Photography by Joseph Ruttenberg. Running time: 94 minutes. An MGM release.

Karin — Greta Garbo
Larry Blake — Melvyn Douglas
Griselda Vaughn — Constance Bennett
O.O. Miller — Roland Young
Dick Williams — Robert Sterling
Miss Ellis — Ruth Gordon
Miss Dunbar — Frances Carson
Dancer — Robert Alton

A woman fears she is losing her husband's affections to his worldly-wise, former girlfriend. The wife then concocts a scheme to divert the man's attentions by posing as her supposed twin sister, turning on a hidden reserve of charm and vivacity and winning him back, albeit to her "new" identity. While the trick appears to be working, the husband discovers the ruse and pursues his "sister-in-law" with alarming determination until the pair drop their pretenses and are reconciled.

This attempt to Americanize Greta Garbo's screen image (wartime embargoes had denied her the faithful European ticket buyers who kept her films profitable) gave her a part more ideally suited to the talents of Irene Dunne, who had become a major screwball performer in just such tales of feigned zaniness and assumed identity. The elegance and mystery of Garbo's previous screen incarnations

Constance Bennett, Melvyn Douglas, Greta Garbo, and Robert Sterling in
Two-Faced Woman, copyright 1941 by Loew's Incorporated.

were totally missing from this new assignment, and the moral controversy the film created, instead of reaping profits by drawing in the
curious, only served to confirm in the public mind that a sacrilege of
sorts had occurred, thereby justifying a consensus of non-attendance.
Although later viewings reveal a fairly entertaining screwball romance (of trickery and pursuit) enhanced by the Metro studio polish,
solid supporting roles, and George Cukor's careful direction, the narrative's initial implication that the husband is willingly attempting
adultery with someone he believes to be his wife's sister aroused the
wrath of the Catholic Church. Condemned in its original release version, *Two-Faced Woman* was fitted with an added scene portraying
the husband as discovering his wife's ruse early on, even though
subsequent scenes appear to contradict this information. Following
the film's box-office failure, MGM made no further screwball comedies; Garbo gave up acting for good.

Ball of Fire

1941. Directed by Howard Hawks. Produced by Samuel Goldwyn. Written by Billy Wilder and Charles Brackett. From story by Billy Wilder and Thomas Monroe. Photography by Gregg Toland. Running time: 111 minutes. A Samuel Goldwyn/United Artists release.

Professor Bertram Potts—Gary Cooper
Sugarpuss O'Shea—Barbara Stanwyck
Professor Gurkakoff—Oscar Homolka
Professor Jerome—Henry Travers
Professor Magenbruch—S.Z. Sakall
Professor Robinson—Tully Marshall
Professor Quintana—Leonid Kinsky
Professor Oddly—Richard Haydn
Professor Peagram—Aubrey Mather
Garbage Man—Allen Jenkins
Joe Lilac—Dana Andrews
Duke Pastrami—Dan Duryea
Asthma Anderson—Ralph Peters
Miss Bragg—Kathleen Howard
Miss Totten—Mary Field
Larsen—Charles Lane
McNeary—Charles Arnt
Waiter—Elisha Cook, Jr.
Themselves—Gene Kupra and His Orchestra

A sexy stripper, on the run from her gangster boyfriend and his henchmen, hides out at a New York brownstone populated by a group of eccentric, mostly middle-aged college professors who have spent the past nine years preparing a new encyclopedia. Her arrival coincides with the youngest team member's tackling the topic of "slang," and the stripper's liberal use of street-smart expressions makes her the ideal subject for further research by the junior faculty member, who also becomes both her new love interest and her rescuer from her criminal pursuers.

Producer Goldwyn's second and final foray into screwball territory (and director Hawks' fourth) hinges on culture-clash and the humorous upset of academic decorum, extending the premise from previous vamp-the-professor comedies to a whole range of peculiar pedants who react to the sensuous intruder's presence in various, non-academic ways. The story, based on an original Billy Wilder screenplay written in Europe some years earlier, was quickly recog-

Barbara Stanwyck and Gary Cooper in *Ball of Fire*, copyright 1941 by Samuel Goldwyn.

nized by the public as a take-off on *Snow White and the Seven Dwarfs*, although the handsome prince (Gary Cooper) starts out as a member of the enclave, the princess (Barbara Stanwyck) is a decidedly less innocent lass then her cartoon counterpart, and the wicked queen has become an urban crime boss (Dana Andrews). This time the familiar screwball premise of the timid male versus the domineering female is totally devoid of the heroine's often scatterbrained wackiness. As Sugarpuss O'Shea, Stanwyck leaves all the customary confusion to her amazed new admirer, Professor Bertram Potts.

Take a Letter, Darling

1942. Directed by Mitchell Leisen. Produced by Fred Kohlmar. Written by Claude Binyon. From story by George Beck. Photography by John Mescal. Running time: 93 minutes. A Paramount release.

A.M. MacGregor—Rosalind Russell
Tom Varney—Fred MacMurray
Jonathan Caldwell—Macdonald Carey
Ethel Caldwell—Constance Moore
G.B. Atwater—Robert Benchley
Bud Newton—Charles Arnt
Uncle George—Cecil Kellaway
Aunt Minnie—Kathleen Howard
Aunt Judy—Margaret Seddon
Moses—Dooley Wilson
Sam—George H. Reed
Sally—Margaret Hayes
Mickey Dowling—Sonny Boy Williams

A lady advertising executive has a practice of hiring male secretary-escorts as a means of assuaging the suspicions of clients' wives that she is looking for more than contracts. Her problem is that each hired man eventually has to be dismissed for getting too familiar with the boss. When her newest "man Friday" fails to repeat the pattern, and courts a wealthy client's sister instead, the flustered executive has to confront her own rising jealousy, which leads to a reluctant romance with the very secretary who first ignored her.

Role-reversal and childish game-playing among the successful key the action and humor in what became the first wartime screwball release (although filmed before Pearl Harbor). The cycle would soon be winding down, as public taste and the mood of the country underwent major shifts in just a few months. The picture was to have been another of Paramount's Claude Binyon-scripted, Claudette Colbert vehicles, with Michell Leisen in place of the director with whom they often worked, Wesley Ruggles. Leisen had also successfully guided Colbert, but in tamer, warmer, romantic comedies. As things worked out, Colbert moved over to a neighboring stage on the Paramount lot to work for Preston Sturges. Then freelance Rosalind Russell was called in for the boss-lady lead, something in which she was beginning to specialize, and her typing in such roles was in turn advanced

Fred MacMurray and Constance Moore in *Take a Letter, Darling,* copyright 1942 by Paramount Pictures Corporation.

by the results. The kind of elaborate hobbies great wealth sometimes subsidizes got a satirical skewering via the bumbling Robert Benchley's characterization of a power-weary executive whom Russell's character is said to have been hired to assist and then actually replace—so he could have more time to play with expensive toys and games.

Lady in a Jam

1942. Directed and produced by Gregory La Cava. Written by Eugene Thackery, Frank Cockrell and Otho Lovering. Photography by Hal Mohr. Running time: 80 minutes. A Universal release.

Jane Palmer—Irene Dunne
Dr. Enright—Patric Knowles
Stanley—Ralph Bellamy

Mr. Billingsley — Eugene Pallette
Dr. Brewster — Samuel S. Hinds
Cactus Kate — Queenie Vassar
Strawberry — Jane Garland
Groundhog — Edward McWade
Faro Bill — Robert Homans

A New York socialite suffers financial reverses which are cushioned only by the unexpected inheritance of an abandoned Arizona mine. Her trip out west is complicated by her legal guardian's insistence that she undergo psychotherapy to cure her of her madcap behavior. Her doctor then discovers the best remedy is marriage — with him.

With the screwball cycle waning and war at the door, Gregory La Cava opted for a drastic change of locale in his next effort, which also was marked by the culmination of his growing practice of improvisational filming. His previous Irene Dunne vehicle for Universal, *Unfinished Business* (1941), was the first of only two screen credits for the mysterious scriptwriter "Eugene Thackery." *Lady in a Jam* was the other, but both were rumored largely to be "made up" by the director and his players as the filming progressed, this time on location in the Mojave Desert. La Cava's firm belief in psychoanalysis received scant missionary support from what resulted, however. Perhaps as a sign that the day of the zany heiress was over, Irene Dunne's familiar character in the film ceases to be a liberating force in the lives of repressed others. Instead, she is clinically identified as a neurotic — and in need of a rational cure. Screwball regulars, such as Eugene Pallette and Ralph Bellamy are still on hand for laughs, few that they are, but the film's most memorable gag comes in the form of a horseback chorus of singing American Indians.

The Major and the Minor

1942. Directed by Billy Wilder. Produced by Arthur Hornblow, Jr. Written by Charles Brackett and Billy Wilder. From play by Edward Childs Carpenter and from story by Fannie Kilbourne. Photography by Leo Tover. Running time: 100 minutes. A Paramount release.

Susan Applegate — Ginger Rogers
Major Kirby — Ray Milland
Pamela Hill — Rita Johnson
Mr. Osborne — Robert Benchley
Lucy Hill — Diana Lynn
Colonel Hill — Edward Fielding
Cadet Osborne — Frankie Thomas
Cadet Wigton — Raymond Roe
Cadet Korner — Charles Smith
Cadet Babcock — Larry Nunn
Cadet Miller — Billy Dawson
Mrs. Applegate — Lela Rogers

A handsome, bachelor officer, taking a wartime train trip to assume a less than exciting new post at a Midwestern, juvenile military academy, befriends what he believes to be a distressed 12-year-old girl and brings her to the school while trying to make arrangements for her care. His growing (and discomforting) attraction to her, and the series of disruptions she sets in motion at the school, are eventually explained to all as inadvertent results of her deception. She is actually a grown woman, trying to return home to Iowa (at half-fare) to escape the wolfish hazards of Manhattan.

Screwball comedy first acknowledged the war effort with this sly entry, providing motivational dialogue for Ray Milland as a desk-bound officer hoping for challenging re-assignment to overseas combat. The picture marked Billy Wilder's being allowed by Paramount brass to follow the successful example of Preston Sturges in moving from the contract writers' building to the director's chair. The upsetting of established propriety characteristics of the genre is transplanted, as was the story in *Lady in a Jam* to a new location far from the world of the New York night club and penthouse, but the often embarrassing effects follow genre custom. Standard too, is the playful aggressiveness in the girl/woman's initially unwelcome flirting with her mild-mannered protector, but here her excuse for childish behavior hinges not on being a wacky debutante or spoiled heiress, but simply (and falsely) on being a mere child. In later years Wilder would joke about getting a risque script, seemingly about repressed pedophilia, past the censors of the day, but it should be remembered that the temporary loosening of the Production Code, to boost domestic industry earnings after the loss of the European market, might also have contributed to why this one got through.

Once Upon a Honeymoon

1942. Directed and produced by Leo McCarey. Written by Sheridan Gibney. From story by Leo McCarey. Photography by George Barnes. Running time: 115 minutes. An RKO release.

Katie O'Hara — Ginger Rogers
Pat O'Toole — Cary Grant
Baron Von Luber — Walter Slezak
Gaston Leblanc — Albert Dekker
Marshall Borelski — Albert Basserman
Elsa — Ferike Boros
Ed Cumberland — Harry Shannon
Anna Beckstein — Natasha Lytess
Tailor — Hans Conreid
German Officer — Lionel Royce
Waiter — Alex Melesh
Baron's Guests — Walter Stahl
              Russell Gaige
Traveler — Dina Smirnova

An American golddigger marries what she thinks is a rich European prospect, only to learn that he is an important Nazi official, and that the ocean liner on which they are to spend their honeymoon is taking her away to virtual captivity in Germany. The bearer of this news is a dapper American journalist who convinces her of her folly and assists her in subverting her hateful husband's plans.

Just as Leo McCarey's years of screwball success paralleled Gregory La Cava's, working with some of the same stars, similar stories, and even similar methods of shooting (improvisation amidst a party atmosphere on the set) — so did their directorial misfires end their participation in the genre as its cycle was about to grind to a wartime halt. The disruption of propriety (a pompous VIP's honeymoon) gives sufficient opportunity for shipboard hi-jinks in first-class settings, but propagandistic speeches and a meandering narrative dilute the comedy's impact. The finished film is surely the longest of all entries in the cycle (nearly two hours) and the grimly humorous ending, with the budding romance between the Americans cleared to proceed by the drowning of the Nazi, is made more difficult to accept lightheartedly than would have been the case if the actor in the part had been a more sober villain than that performed by comic bad-guy Walter Slezak. The historically anarchic spirit of screwball perhaps could have been mated to patriotic indoctrination in some more effective way, but the impression of *Once Upon a Honeymoon* is that it would be a nearly impossible task.

I Married a Witch

1942. Directed and produced by Rene Clair. Written by Robert Pirosh and Marc Connelly. From novel by Thorne Smith and Norman Matson. Photography by Ted Tetzlaff. Special effects by Gordon Jennings. Running time: 76 minutes. A Paramount/United Artists release.

Wallace Wooley—Fredric March
Jennifer—Veronica Lake
Dr. Dudley White—Robert Benchley
Estelle Masterson—Susan Hayward
Daniel—Cecil Kellaway
Margaret—Elizabeth Patterson
J.B. Masterson—Robert Warwick
Tabitha—Ely Maylon
Town Crier—Robert Greig
Vocalist—Helen St. Rayner
Justice of Peace—Aldrich Bowker
J.P.'s Wife—Emma Dunn
Martha—Viola Moore
Nancy—Mary Field
Harriet—Nora Cecil
Allen—Emory Parnell
Rufus—Charles Moore
Prison Guard—Al Bridge
Guest—Arthur Stuart Hull
Bartender—Chester Conklin
Young Man—Reed Hadley

A beautiful young witch and her mischievous, warlock father are burned at the stake in 1690 Salem, Massachusetts. Her curse upon the family of the man who denounced her (that he and all his male descendants will have unhappy marriages) comes true until the present day, when a bolt of lightning frees the spirits of the father and daughter from an ancient tree stump at the sight of their fiery execution. The daughter then decides to extend the curse personally by materializing as a modern woman who creates romantic problems for its latest victim, a stuffy, prestigious, candidate for governor. The pretty witch's malicious plans are exorcised when her spite for the man turns to love (stronger than witchcraft), and the marriage referred to in the title results.

As the colorful parade of screwball comedy's eccentric, man-chasing women neared its conclusion amid the suddenly shifting social values of "the duration," this charming, special-effects laced, battle of the sexes appeared under the guidance of a famous French refugee who had successfully dealt with the lighter side of the unreal in his European productions, Rene Clair. With the doors of Paramount opened to him by the admiring Preston Sturges, Clair strove to give Thorne Smith's final novel (completed by Norman Matson) just the appropriate touch of earnest whimsy it deserved, while not losing sight of the screwball potential in the witch's initial resentment and growing attraction toward her mortal victim. The fact that his character is a judge adds to the sense of personal austerity and dignity being overturned by the meddling heroine, who in this case has genuine magical powers at her disposal, although she prefers to employ a more common (and comely) set of feminine wiles while making him a fool for love. Related comedies in the genre sometimes used a more mundanely empowered female, such as a lady boss or executive secretary, to manipulate a weak male, before domesticating him. Here the aggressive woman sets out to ruin, rather than win, her target — and is herself tamed by the all-too-human emotion sparked by the relationship she conjures up with him. There may have been something of "the witch" in many of her screwball predecessors in the cycle, as they often drove their hapless men to the brink of desperation, but now the transformation is total and the female mindset has switched from daffy to diabolical. Even so, love conquers the powers of darkness in time for a convention-abiding, happy ending.

The Palm Beach Story

1942. Directed by Preston Sturges. Produced by Paul Jones. Written by Preston Sturges. Photography by Victor Milner. Running time: 88 minutes. A Paramount release.

Gerry Jeffers—Claudette Colbert
Tom Jeffers—Joel McCrea
Princess—Mary Astor
John D. Hackensacker III—Rudy Vallee
Toto—Sig Arno
Mr. Hinch—Robert Warwick
Mr. Osmond—Arthur Stuart Hull
Dr. Kluck—Torben Meyer
Mr. Asweld—Jimmy Conlin
Mr. McKeewie—Vic Potel
The Wienie King—Robert Dudley
Manager—Franklin Pangborn
Pullman Conductor—Arthur Hoyt
Conductor—Al Bridge
Bartender—Snowflake
Porter—Charles Moore
Brakeman—Frank Moran
Orchestra Leader—Harry Rosenthal
Wienie King's Wife—Esther Howard
Ale & Quail Club—William Demarest
                Jack Norton, Robert Greig
                Roscoe Ates, Dewey Robinson
                Chester Conklin, Sheldon Jett

Rudy Vallee, Joel McCrea, and Claudette Colbert in *The Palm Beach Story*, copyright 1942 by Paramount Pictures Corporation.

The wife of a failed architect-inventor decides to leave her husband and take up golddigging, reasoning that he would have a better chance at success if he were single and she were able to snare a rich, new boyfriend. Her drastic decision is followed by a kismet-like bestowing of cash from a wizened, "wienie-king" (a filthy-rich sausage packer), plus a wild, slapstick adventure with an inebriated group of wealthy sportsmen (the "Ale and Quail Club") on board a train bound for the Florida playground of the rich. En route she succeeds in gaining the attentions of a prissy, bachelor millionaire who buys her a new wardrobe and invites her to vacation in Palm Beach with him and his much-married sister. The deserted inventor-husband tracks his wayward spouse to the Florida resort, only to be introduced as her "brother" to the millionaire's sister, who then pursues the "brother" as a potentially new conquest. A happy ending is facilitated by the revelation that the estranged couple, although now reconciled, both have unmarried, identical twins, who subsequently marry the wealthy siblings.

Scheduled to begin production just a month before Pearl Harbor, *The Palm Beach Story* helped, upon release, to ring down the curtain on the screwball cycle. While part of the film is pointed parody aimed at the Florida-vacationing, moneybags crowd into whose circles author-director Sturges once disastrously tried to marry, the narrative's broader relation to the bulk of screwball comedy is also clear. Claudette Colbert, who replaced the intended Carole Lombard just before shooting began, caps her screwball career with yet another dollar-hungry characterization, again wholly devoid of either zaniness or naïveté, as the aggressive female who sets the plot wheels in motion while passive males dance to her tune and lose all the verbal sparring matches. Her character's romantic reunion with her husband, ironically enacted against an old-fashioned serenade (below a balcony) performed by her unaware, wealthy suitor (Rudy Vallee), at first seems to be a surprising lapse in the monetary practicality which she has championed, but the incredible surprise of substituting her and her husband's twins in the newly cultivated affairs of the plot lets true dollar value reign supreme. Still, Sturges does not leave well enough alone after having kidded and pushed the screwball conventions to such a fantastic extreme. The "and they lived happily ever after" cliché, overtly questioned in a printed title at the narrative's opening, provided motivation for what became a flashback plot. The same title returns on screen at the film's close, only to have its physical manifestation (inscribed in script upon a supposed sheet of before-the-camera glass) shattered off screen, via a crashing sound effect symbolizing both the camera's collision with it, in the process of a dolly shot, and the shattering of the illusion implied by the "happy endings" of all previous screwball comedies, wherein formerly combative, opposite character types appear to be headed for bliss—despite their unresolved differences in temperament and the inevitable, conformist pressures of even the make-believe society on screen, which flatteringly mirrors the harsher one beyond the box office window.

Conclusion

As a pure cinematic form, historically limited at opposite ends of a time continuum by New Deal optimism and Pearl Harbor mobilization, the classical screwball comedy ends here, on a self-reflexive note of gleeful recognition of its wild improbability. Sturges kept his verbally dense version of its pacing alive in a few subsequent films, but they were topical satires aimed at the new era—wartime America. Heiresses, tycoons, golddiggers, scatterbrains, and bookish bachelors need not apply out of uniform. After the war, Hawks too, managed a few postscripts to the wonderful, bygone cycle, but the boat had sailed, and they were fated to be mainly nostalgia items, quite out of tune with society's later preoccupations and penchants.

A generation of film-school students would, much later, study key works of the screwball cycle much as academically trained playwrights or novelists of the modern era learn to analyze, say, Restoration comedy or the nineteenth-century realist novel. The mini-wave of pseudo-screwball, 1970s sex comedies, which overlapped into the following decade with modest effect, can be attributed in part to such schooling—and to the time-tested desire to steal from the best. But warming over the conventions of a lost time, without the censorial, economic, and political vectors of the actual period to shape the product, has proven to be an exercise in *hommage* more than in artistry. It is to the genuine item that this reference work is directed, with the hope that a contextual perspective on its rise and fall will be of benefit to the serious researcher or committed visitor to this splendidly entertaining chapter of the movie past.

NOTES

1. Andrew Sarris, "The Sex Comedy Without Sex," *American Film*, March 1978, pp. 8–15.

2. Stanley Cavell, *Pursuits of Happiness: The Hollywood Comedy of Remarriage*. Cambridge, Mass.: Harvard University Press, 1981.

3. David Thompson, *A Biographical Dictionary of Film*. New York: William Morrow, 1976, pp. 218–219.

4. David Shipman, *The Great Movie Stars: The Golden Years*. New York: Bonanza, 1970, pp. 173–175.

5. Wes Gehring, *Screwball Comedy: A Genre of Madcap Romance*. New York: Greenwood Press, 1986, pp. 143–144.

6. Shipman, pp. 173–175.

7. Gehring, pp. 134–139.

8. Thompson, pp. 344–346.

9. Shipman, pp. 22–25.

10. Herman Mankiewicz as quoted by Jeffrey Brown Martin, *Ben Hecht: Hollywood Screenwriter*. Ann Arbor, Mich.: UMI Research Press, 1985, p. 488.

11. Pauline Kael, "Raising Kane," *The Citizen Kane Book*. Boston: Little, Brown, 1971.

12. Martin, p. 25.

13. Martin, p. 27.

14. Irene Watkins, "Norman Krasna," *Dictionary of Literary Biography*. Detroit: Gale, 1984, p. 187.

15. Norman Krasna as quoted by Pat McGilligan, *Backstory: Interviews with Screenwriters of Hollywood's Golden Age*. Los Angeles: University of California Press, 1986, p. 221.

16. Gehring, pp. 51–55.

17. Paramount Studio Biography, "Claude Binyon," February 10, 1939.

18. Capt. Claude Binyon, "How to Write a Motion Picture," *Daily Variety*, January 3, 1945, p. 24.

19. Larry May, *Screening Out the Past: The Birth of Mass Culture and the Motion Picture Industry*. New York: Oxford University Press, 1980, pp. 147–166.

20. Frank Capra, *The Name Above the Title.* New York: Macmillan, 1971, p. 159–167.

21. Ibid.

22. Andrew Bergman, *We're In the Money: Depression America and Its Films.* New York: Harper and Row, 1971, 132–148.

23. Robin Wood, *Howard Hawks.* Garden City, N.Y.: Doubleday, 1968, pp. 11–12.

24. Leland A. Poague, *The Hollywood Professionals: Volume 7.* New York: A.S. Barnes, 1980, p. 309.

25. Gehring, p. 99–107.

26. James Ursini, *Preston Sturges: An American Dreamer.* New York: Curtis Books, 1973, p. 61.

27. Manny Farber and W.S. Poster, "Preston Sturges: Success in the Movies," *Film Culture,* Winter, 1962.

28. James Curtis, *Between Flops: A Biography of Preston Sturges.* New York: Harcourt Brace Jovanovich, 1982, pp. 269–277.

BIBLIOGRAPHY

Bergman, Andrew. *We're In the Money.* New York: Harper & Row, 1971.

Binyon, Capt. Claude. "How to Write a Motion Picture," *Daily Variety,* January 3, 1945.

Capra, Frank. *Frank Capra: The Name Above the Title.* New York: Macmillan, 1971.

Cavell, Stanley. *Pursuits of Happiness: The Hollywood Comedy of Remarriage.* Cambridge, Mass.: Harvard University Press, 1981.

Corliss, Richard, ed. *The Hollywood Screenwriters.* New York: Avon, 1970.

_____. *Talking Pictures.* New York: Overlook, 1974.

Curtis, James. *Between Flops: A Biography of Preston Sturges.* New York: Harcourt Brace Jovanovich, 1982.

Dooley, Roger. *From Scarface to Scarlet.* New York: Harcourt Brace Jovanovich, 1981.

Durgnat, Raymond. *The Crazy Mirror.* New York: Horizon, 1970.

Farber, Manny, and W.S. Poster. "Preston Sturges: Success in the Movies." *Film Culture,* Film Culture. Winter, 1962.

Ferguson, Otis. "While We Were Laughing" (1940). In *The Film Criticism of Otis Ferguson.* Edited by Robert Wilson. Philadelphia: Temple University Press, 1971.

Fine, Richard. *Hollywood and the Profession of Authorship.* Ann Arbor, Mich.: UMI Research Press, 1985.

Gehring, Wes. *Screwball Comedy: A Genre of Madcap Romance.* New York: Greenwood Press, 1986.

_____. "Screwball Comedy: An Overview." *Journal of Popular Film and Television.* Winter, 1985.

_____. *Screwball Comedy: Defining a Film Genre.* Muncie, Indiana: Ball State University Monographs, 1983.

Griffith, Richard, and Arthur Mayer. *The Movies.* New York: Simon and Schuster, 1957.

Hagen, Ray. "The Day of the Runaway Heiress." *Films and Filming.* April, 1966.

Harris, Warren G. *Cary Grant: A Touch of Elegance.* Garden City, N.Y.: Doubleday, 1987.

Harvey, James. *Romantic Comedy*. New York: Alfred A. Knopf, 1987.
Haskell, Molly. *From Reverence to Rape*. New York: Holt, Rinehart and Winston, 1974.
Hecht, Ben. *A Child of the Century*. New York: Simon and Schuster, 1954.
Henderson, Brian. "Romantic Comedy Today: Semi-Tough or Impossible?" *Film Quarterly*. Summer, 1978.
Higham, Charles. *Kate: The Life of Katharine Hepburn*. New York: Signet, 1975.
Jacobs, Lewis. *The Rise of the American Film*. New York: Teachers College Press, 1971, orig. pub. 1939.
Kael, Pauline. "Raising Kane." *The Citizen Kane Book*. Boston: Little, Brown, 1971.
Kaminsky, Stuart M. *American Film Genres*. Dayton: Pflaum, 1974.
Kay, Karyn. "Controversy and Correspondence." *Film Quarterly*. Summer, 1976.
————. "Part-Time Work of a Domestic Slave." *Film Quarterly*. Fall 1975.
Knight, Arthur. *The Liveliest Art*. New York: McMillan, 1957.
Leach, Jim. "Screwball Comedy." *Film Genre*. ed. Barry K. Grant. Metuchen, N.J.: Scarecrow, 1977.
McCaffrey, Donald W. *The Golden Age of Sound Comedy*. New York: A.S. Barnes, 1973.
McGilligan, Pat. *Backstory: Interviews with Screenwriters of Hollywood's Golden Age*. Los Angeles: University of California Press, 1987.
Magill, Frank N., ed. *Magill's American Film Guide*. Englewood Cliffs, N.J.: Salem, 1980.
Maltin, Leonard. *Carole Lombard*. New York: Pyramid, 1976.
Marill, Alvin H. *Samuel Goldwyn Presents*. Cranbury, N.J.: A.S. Barnes, 1976.
Martin, Jeffrey Brown. *Ben Hecht: Hollywood Screenwriter*. Ann Arbor, Mich.: UMI Research Press, 1985.
Mast, Gerald. *The Comic Mind*. Indianapolis: Bobbs-Merrill, 1973.
May, Larry. *Screening Out the Past: The Birth of Mass Culture and the Motion Picture Industry*. New York: Oxford University Press, 1980.
Palmer, Jerry. *The Logic of the Absurd*. London: British Film Institute, 1987.
Paramount Studio Biography. "Claude Binyon." February 10, 1939.
Poague, Leland A. "Controversy and Correspondence." *Film Quarterly*. Summer, 1976.
————. *The Hollywood Professionals: Volume 7*. San Diego: A.S. Barnes, 1980.
Rubenstein, E. "The End of Screwball Comedy: The Lady Eve and the Palm Beach Story." *Post Script*. Spring/Summer, 1982.
Sarris, Andrew. "La Cava: Weirdness and Whoopie." *Village Voice*. July 13, 1981.
————. "The Sex Comedy Without Sex." *American Film*. March, 1978.
————. "The World of Howard Hawks." *Films and Filming*. July–August, 1962.
Schatz, Thomas. *Hollywood Genres: Formulas, Filmmaking, and the Studio System*. Philadelphia: Temple University Press, 1981.

Schmidt, Sanford Michael. *The Theme of Class Confrontation in Hollywood's Romantic Comedies, 1934–1942.* Ph.D. Dissertation, New York University, 1978.

Sennett, Ted. *Lunatics and Lovers.* New Rochelle: Arlington House, 1973.

Silver, Charles. "Leo McCarey: From Marx to McCarthy." *Film Comment.* September, 1973.

Spoto, Donald. *The Art of Alfred Hitchcock.* New York: Hopkinson and Blake, 1976.

Taylor, John Russell. *Hitch.* New York: Pantheon, 1978.

Thomaier, William. "Early Sound Comedy Was Influenced by the Instability of the '30s and Was Therefore Screwball." *Films in Review.* May 1958.

Ursini, James. *Preston Sturges: An American Dreamer.* New York: Curtis Books, 1973.

Watkins, Irene. "Norman Krasna." *Dictionary of Literary Biography.* Detroit: Gale, 1984.

Weales, Gerald. *Canned Goods as Caviar: American Film Comedy of the 1930s.* Chicago: University of Chicago Press, 1985.

Wood, Robin. *Howard Hawks.* Garden City, N.Y.: Doubleday, 1968.

Zolotow, Maurice. *Billy Wilder in Hollywood.* New York: G.P. Putnam's Sons, 1977.

Most useful of the above sources were those works which concentrated upon either defining screwball comedy, so as to set it apart from other types of film humor, or explaining its function from a historical perspective. Wes Gehring's work on the topic was a primary inspiration and critical guide for this reference book. Gehring, who has made the study of 1930s film comedy his life's work, traces the major trends in American humor up to the darkest days of the Depression and notes a significant shift in pre-eminence from the "crackerbarrel," satirical joking of Will Rogers to the comically antiheroic behavior of Cary Grant, Melvyn Douglas, or Fred MacMurray, reacting to the sex-role-reversing, aggressively daffy machinations of Katharine Hepburn, Irene Dunne, or Carole Lombard. Gehring's detective work into comedy's past and his meticulous relating of screwball's practitioners make him the unquestioned authority in this field.

While Gehring applies the rigor of a scholar to define the genre as a movement in the history of popular culture, James Harvey devotes the lifelong energy of a highly literate fan to a lengthy series of close readings of both screwball and conventionally romantic films. But Harvey's insights into the fictional characters, their apparent motivations, and the historical framework of the film industry which gave them screen life, are not the only important features of his book. He also devotes much copy to his unique and intense appreciation of the performers and creators of movie romance in the last two decades before television.

Another inveterate film viewer with impressive powers of retention is Roger Dooley, whose attempt to encapsulate the whole of Hollywood's 1930s output between two covers tends to rely upon citing plot formulas in order to forge a structure out of such a massive undertaking. Dooley's identification of the various approaches to screwball is only a minor part of his prodigious work, but it forms an intersting cross-check on possibilities for study with the earlier volume by Ted Sennett, which despite its overt identification as a book about screwball, reaches out very broadly to plot-summarize a much wider variety of movie comedy in the pre–TV years.

The encyclopedic layman's approach to identifying screwball comedy gives way to more formal categorization in three books which concentrate on fixing genre study as a viable avenue of academic film studies. While Stuart M. Kaminsky prefers the term "man-woman" comedy and focuses on the battle of the sexes variation of screwball, Thomas Schatz sets screwball as a cycle of films not only flowing from the Frank Capra innovation of 1934, but also with most of Capra's subsequent films continuing and expanding the genre. Jim Leach's essay in the Barry K. Grant-edited anthology concentrates on the importance of a workable methodology for genre definition, using screwball comedy as a pitfall-prone model.

Early attempts to define and appreciate the screwball film date from the seminal essays of Lewis Jacobs and Otis Ferguson, both of which reveal how clearly the cycle stood out from other forms of movie comedy even when these films were in current production. Historical placement of screwball built upon these early definitions a generation later, as is evident in the 1950s writings of William Thomaier, Arthur Knight, and the team of Richard Griffith and Arthur Mayer. Ray Hagen's article on "runaway heiresses" constituted the scant critical/historical attention paid to the cycle in the 1960s, but in the next decade came Andrew Bergman's sociological view of Depression-era Hollywood, with Frank Capra presented as both a father and major practitioner of screwball.

While the majority of the studies of Capra tend to view him from other perspectives, auteurist examinations of Howard Hawks (by Andrew Sarris and Robin Wood), Leo McCarey (by Charles Silver, Leland Poague and Wes Gehring), and Preston Sturges (by Manny Farber/W.S. Poster, James Ursini and James Curtis) readily acknowledge these filmmakers' contributions to the screwball vision. The 1981 Gregory La Cava article by Andrew Sarris is simply insufficient; a full-length book on La Cava is long overdue. Following the 1971 uproar over Pauline Kael's linking the verbal excellence of many 1930s comedies to an overlooked newspaper/magazine tradition which traveled west with the best of Broadway in 1929, attention to the screenwriter's contribution to screwball comedy finally arrived with the publication of books by Richard Corliss, Richard Fine, and Pat McGilligan.

The difficulties in attempting a modern-era appreciation of the social/sexual values inherent in screwball comedy are most apparent in the exchange of journal correspondence by Karen Kay and Leland Poague. These letters are best read in the distancing light of historical perspective offered on screwball by Molly Haskell in her study of women in film and by Andrew Sarris in his article on the genre's emergence from a tightening of Hollywood self-censorship.

A curious narrowing, to the point of constricting, approach to screwball comedy can be found in Stanley Cavell's book. Despite the widespread use of the term "screwball" to describe these films over half a century of repeated screenings and critiques, Cavell deliberately refuses the label in favor of placing six of the pictures, plus one not generally known as such, in his invented category of "remarriage" comedies. His analysis of their comic form and substance then proceeds with masterly aplomb as he identifies their descent from profound historic lines of thought in the evolution of western culture. Cavell succeeds in giving the anarchic world of screwball a fine pedigree indeed. Gerald Weales' close study of a handful of 1930s comedies, unlike Cavell, does not limit itself to screwball, but does present it as a prime example of the varied ways in which the film humor of that decade has attained classic status. More general surveys of film comedy which pay useful attention to the screwball tradition, even when not calling it by that name, include books by Gerald Mast, Raymond Durgnat, and Donald W. McCaffrey, the last of which is particularly interesting in its study of screwball titles overlooked by most other writers.

INDEX

Entries with page numbers in **boldface** indicate filmography entries. Page numbers in *italics* refer to illustrations.